Business Psychology and Sales

Hemant Bansal

FanatiXx Publication

FanatiXx® Publication
AM/56, Basanti Colony, Rourkela 769012, Odisha
ISO 9001:2015 Certified

© Copyright, 2025 Hemant Bansal

All rights reserved. No part of this book may be reproduced, stored in a retrieval system, or transmitted, in any form by any means, electronic, mechanical, magnetic, optical, chemical, manual, photocopying, recording, or otherwise, without the prior written consent of the author.

By: Hemant Bansal

ISBN: 978-93-5605-373-1

Book: Business Psychology and Sales
Price: INR 199/-

Printing By: BooksClub.in
The opinions/ contents expressed in this book are the sole of the author and do not represent the opinions/ stands/ thoughts of FanatiXx® or any of its associates and affiliations.

Contents

Introduction .... *ix*

Chapter 1 : Understanding Business Psychology *1*

   1.1 The Intersection of Psychology and Business 1

   1.2 The Role of Psychology in Sales 2

   1.3 Key Psychological Principles for Effective Selling 3

   1.4 The Psychological Foundations of Building Customer Relationships 5

   1.5 How to Apply Business Psychology to Improve Sales Performance 6

Chapter 2 : Consumer Motivation and Needs *8*

   2.1 What Drives Consumer Decisions? 8

   2.2 Maslow's Hierarchy of Needs in Sales 9

   2.3 The Psychology of Wants vs. Needs 10

   2.4 The Role of Pain Points in Consumer Motivation 11

   2.5 Tapping Into Emotional Triggers 13

   2.6 Identifying and Tapping Into Customer Needs 14

Chapter 3 : The Psychology of Influence and Persuasion in Sales *16*

   3.1 The Science of Influence 16

   3.2 The Role of Trust in Persuasion 20

   3.3 The Power of Emotional Appeal 21

   3.4 Overcoming Objections with Persuasion Techniques 22

   3.5 Ethical Persuasion in Sales 24

Chapter 4 : The Role of Personality in Sales Success............26

4.1 Why Personality Matters in Sales...26

4.2 Personality Models in Sales 27

4.3 Adapting Sales Approaches to Different Personality Types .30

4.4 The Salesperson's Personality and Its Impact on Sales 32

4.5 Personality Conflicts in Sales...34

Chapter 5 : Emotional Intelligence in Sales...................................36

5.1 Understanding Emotional Intelligence (EI).........................36

5.2 The Importance of Emotional Intelligence in Sales 37

5.3 Developing Emotional Intelligence in Sales 39

5.4 Emotional Intelligence in Handling Difficult Customers.....40

5.5 Emotional Triggers in Sales 42

Chapter 6 : Building Rapport and Trust in Sales..........................44

6.1 The Importance of Rapport and Trust in Sales.....................44

6.2 Techniques for Building Rapport 45

6.3 Strategies for Establishing Trust..47

6.4 Maintaining Rapport and Trust Over Time 49

Chapter 7 : Effective Communication Skills in Sales...................53

7.1 The Role of Communication in Sales..................................53

7.2 Key Communication Skills for Sales 54

7.3 Adapting Communication Styles...57

7.4 Handling Difficult Conversations..58

Chapter 8 : Understanding Customer Behavior and Decision-Making 61

8.1 The Importance of Understanding Customer Behavior 61

8.2 Factors Influencing Customer Behavior 62

8.3 The Customer Decision-Making Process............................. 64

8.4 Leveraging Customer Behavior Insights in Sales................ 65

Chapter 9 : Advanced Negotiation Skills in Sales 68

9.1 The Art of Negotiation in Sales 68

9.2 Psychological Principles Behind Effective Negotiation 69

9.3 Managing Buyer Resistance and Objections 70

9.4 The Power of Reciprocity and Concessions 71

9.5 How to Read Non-Verbal Cues in Negotiations 72

9.6 High-Pressure Sales Situations: Staying Calm and Strategic 73

9.7 Closing Deals: When and How to Seal the Agreement 73

Chapter 10 : The Psychology of Consumer Decision-Making..... 76

10.1 Understanding the Consumer Decision-Making Process .. 76

10.2 The Role of Cognitive Biases in Consumer Choices.......... 77

10.3 How Emotions Influence Purchases 78

10.4 The Impact of Social Proof on Buying Behavior............... 79

10.5 Building a Persuasive Argument for Buyers...................... 80

10.6 Decision Fatigue: How to Simplify Choices 81

10.7 The Post-Purchase Decision: Building Customer Loyalty 82

Chapter 11 : Cross-Cultural Sales Psychology...........................83

11.1 Understanding Cultural Differences in Sales Psychology ..83

11.2 Cultural Norms and Their Impact on Buying Behavior 84

11.3 Adapting Sales Approaches for Different Markets.............85

11.4 Cross-Cultural Communication in Sales 86

11.5 Building Trust Across Cultures..87

11.6 Tailoring Emotional Appeals for International Audiences..87

11.7 Global vs. Local: Striking the Right Balance in Sales Strategies 88

11.8 Case Studies of Successful Cross-Cultural Sales Campaigns...89

Chapter 12 : Leveraging Technology and Data in Sales..............91

12.1 The Role of Technology in Sales..91

12.2 Utilizing Data Analytics in Sales..92

12.3 Personalizing Sales Interactions with Technology 94

12.4 Embracing Emerging Technologies.....................................96

12.5 Implementing Technology and Data in Your Sales Strategy 97

Chapter 13 : Building and Managing a High-Performance Sales Team..99

13.1 Understanding the High-Performance Sales Team..............99

13.2 Recruitment Strategies for Building a High-Performance Sales Team..100

13.3 Training and Development for Sales Excellence...............101

13.4 Performance Management in Sales Teams.......................102

13.5 Fostering a Positive Sales Culture 103

13.6 Adapting to Change and Challenges 104

Chapter 14 : Sales Strategy Development and Implementation 106

14.1 Understanding Sales Strategy 106

14.2 Conducting Market Analysis 107

14.3 Identifying Target Audiences 108

14.4 Crafting a Compelling Value Proposition 109

14.5 Developing Sales Tactics and Execution Plans 109

14.6 Monitoring and Measuring Performance 110

14.7 Adapting to Market Changes 111

Chapter 15 : Leveraging Technology in Sales 113

15.1 Understanding Sales Technology 113

15.2 Types of Sales Technologies 114

15.3 Implementing Sales Technology 116

15.4 Best Practices for Leveraging Sales Technology 117

15.5 Future Trends in Sales Technology 118

Chapter 16 : The Future of Sales: Trends and Predictions 121

16.1 Current Trends Influencing Sales 121

16.2 Emerging Technologies in Sales 122

16.3 Predictions for the Future of Sales 123

16.4 Adapting to Change: Strategies for Sales Teams 125

Appendices *127*

   Appendix A: Glossary of Psychological and Sales Terms........127

   Appendix B: Additional Readings and Resources for Further Learning 128

   Appendix C: Useful Sales Psychology Tools and Techniques .130

References *132*

Introduction

In today's fast-paced and highly competitive marketplace, success is no longer just about the quality of your product or service—it's about understanding people. At the heart of every business transaction is human behavior, influenced by a complex blend of emotions, perceptions, and motivations. Whether you're selling software, luxury goods, or consulting services, the psychology behind why people buy is just as important as the product itself. Welcome to *Business Psychology and Sales*, a book that bridges the gap between psychological insights and effective sales strategies.

This book is not merely about closing deals or making quick sales; it's about building long-lasting relationships by understanding the psychological needs of customers. Every interaction a salesperson has—from the first impression to the final handshake—carries psychological weight. Knowing how to tap into these human behaviors can significantly increase sales success, improve customer loyalty, and create a sales culture that thrives in today's dynamic business environment.

Why Business Psychology Matters in Sales

Why do customers say "yes" to one salesperson and "no" to another, even when the products are similar? What drives a customer to make a buying decision based on emotion rather than logic? The answer lies in psychology.

The best sales professionals aren't just product experts—they are people experts. They understand that sales is not just a transactional process, but a relationship built on trust, influence, and emotional intelligence. Through this book, you will explore the deep connections between psychology and sales, learning how to apply these principles to shape consumer behavior and drive sales growth.

Understanding business psychology allows you to:

- Influence customer decisions more effectively.
- Overcome objections with a deeper understanding of customer concerns.
- Build authentic relationships that create loyal, long-term customers.
- Adapt to the psychological shifts brought on by technology and data-driven sales environments.

What You'll Learn

Business Psychology and Sales is divided into five parts, each designed to cover key aspects of the intersection between psychology and sales. You will learn:

- **The psychological foundations of buying behavior**: Understanding how consumers think, feel, and make decisions will enable you to tailor your sales approach to their needs and preferences.
- **Influence and persuasion techniques**: Learn practical, ethical ways to persuade customers using proven psychological principles, from the power of social proof to the role of emotional intelligence.
- **Sales strategies grounded in human behavior**: Master advanced strategies for overcoming resistance, handling objections, and closing deals while maintaining trust and rapport.

- **Motivating and leading sales teams**: Explore how psychological insights can transform sales team performance, from designing effective incentives to fostering resilience and grit in your team members.
- **Future trends in sales psychology**: Get ahead of the curve by understanding how emerging technologies like AI are reshaping the sales landscape through behavioral insights and personalization.

The Human Element in Sales

In this book, you will discover that the best salespeople don't just sell—they understand the human element. They know how to read body language, listen actively, and respond to the unspoken needs of their customers. You will learn how to develop these skills, building trust with customers and leading your sales team to success.

This book is designed for both experienced sales professionals looking to refine their approach and newcomers eager to build a strong foundation in business psychology. Through actionable insights, real-world examples, and practical techniques, you'll gain the tools you need to succeed in any sales environment, regardless of industry or market conditions.

Closing Thoughts

The world of sales is evolving, driven by technological advances, shifting consumer expectations, and new economic realities. Yet, the one constant in this evolution is human psychology. By mastering the psychological principles that underpin effective selling, you can stay ahead of the competition, foster deeper customer relationships, and achieve sustainable business success.

As you journey through *Business Psychology and Sales*, you will uncover the powerful ways psychology shapes every aspect of the sales process. Whether you are closing deals or leading a team, this understanding will empower you to make smarter, more strategic decisions that benefit both your business and your customers.

Let's begin the journey into the fascinating world of business psychology and transform the way you sell.

Chapter 1
Understanding Business Psychology

In the world of business, the ability to understand human behavior is a crucial skill that can separate successful companies and sales professionals from those who struggle. Business psychology is the study of how people think, feel, and act in the business environment. It involves applying psychological principles to business problems, such as understanding consumer behavior, improving employee performance, and increasing the effectiveness of sales strategies.

This chapter will provide a foundation for understanding business psychology and its critical role in the sales process. We'll explore why psychology matters in sales, key psychological principles relevant to business, and how a deeper understanding of human behavior can lead to better sales results.

1.1 The Intersection of Psychology and Business

Psychology has traditionally been the study of the mind, focusing on how individuals think, behave, and interact with the world around them. When applied to business, psychology helps us understand how these same mental processes affect decision-making, consumer behavior, and interpersonal relationships within the marketplace.

Business psychology is more than just understanding customer behavior; it also encompasses the dynamics of leadership, organizational culture, and employee motivation. In sales, psychology is the guiding force behind how we communicate with customers, build relationships, and influence their decisions.

Key Areas Where Psychology Impacts Business:

- **Consumer Behavior**: Understanding the reasons why consumers make purchasing decisions, from rational evaluations to emotional responses.

- **Sales Techniques**: Utilizing psychological insights to build rapport, overcome objections, and close sales more effectively.

- **Leadership and Motivation**: Applying psychological principles to lead sales teams, motivate employees, and foster a healthy work culture.

- **Customer Retention and Loyalty**: Building long-term relationships with customers through trust and emotional engagement.

Business psychology provides the tools needed to address these areas, helping sales professionals become more effective in their roles.

1.2 The Role of Psychology in Sales

At the heart of every sale is a psychological exchange. When a customer buys a product or service, they are not only exchanging money for value but are also making decisions based on their thoughts, emotions, and perceptions. Understanding these underlying psychological processes can give salespeople a competitive edge.

How Psychology Drives the Sales Process:

- **Emotions Influence Decisions**: While customers may believe their decisions are based on logic, emotions often play a more significant role. Sales professionals who can tap into these emotions—whether it's excitement, fear of missing out, or the need for security—can more effectively influence the buying decision.

- **Cognitive Biases Shape Perception**: Human beings rely on mental shortcuts, known as cognitive biases, to make decisions quickly. These biases can impact how customers perceive value, risk, and trustworthiness. Understanding common biases such as the **anchoring effect** (where customers rely heavily on the first piece of information they receive) or the **scarcity effect** (where limited availability increases perceived value) can be pivotal in closing deals.

- **Trust and Relationship Building**: In sales, trust is everything. Without trust, customers are unlikely to make purchases, even if the product or service is a perfect fit. Psychology helps explain how trust is built and maintained, and why rapport is essential in closing high-value deals. Customers are more likely to buy from people they feel connected to and trust.

1.3 Key Psychological Principles for Effective Selling

Several key psychological principles have been identified as particularly relevant in the sales process. By understanding and applying these principles, sales professionals can enhance their ability to persuade, influence, and close deals.

1.3.1 Reciprocity

The principle of reciprocity states that people are more likely to give back when something is given to them. This is a powerful tool in sales. By offering something of value to the customer first—whether it's a free consultation, a discount, or useful information—salespeople can activate the reciprocity effect, making the customer more inclined to reciprocate by making a purchase.

1.3.2 Social Proof

Humans are inherently social creatures who look to others for guidance on how to behave. This is the basis of social proof. In sales, social proof can take the form of testimonials, reviews, or case studies showing how other customers have benefited from the product or service. Highlighting the experiences of satisfied customers can reduce hesitation and increase trust in the salesperson and the offering.

1.3.3 Scarcity

The scarcity principle suggests that people are more likely to desire something when they believe it is in limited supply. Sales professionals can use this principle by emphasizing limited-time offers or highlighting the scarcity of the product. The fear of missing out (FOMO) can be a powerful motivator in driving sales.

1.3.4 Authority

People tend to follow the advice of experts. Establishing authority in sales can be achieved through credentials, certifications, or years of experience in the industry. Salespeople who position themselves as experts are more likely to gain trust and influence the customer's decision-making process.

1.3.5 Commitment and Consistency

People prefer to act in ways that are consistent with their previous commitments. Once a customer has committed to a small action (like signing up for a newsletter or attending a demo), they are more likely to commit to a larger action, like making a purchase. Salespeople can use this principle by encouraging small, low-risk commitments early in the sales process.

1.4 The Psychological Foundations of Building Customer Relationships

A key aspect of business psychology is relationship-building, particularly in sales where long-term success often hinges on the strength of the relationship between the salesperson and the customer. Building these relationships requires an understanding of both emotional intelligence and trust.

Emotional Intelligence in Sales

Emotional intelligence (EQ) refers to the ability to recognize and manage one's own emotions and the emotions of others. Sales professionals with high emotional intelligence are more adept at:

- Reading the emotional states of their customers.
- Responding empathetically to customer needs and concerns.
- Adjusting their sales approach based on the emotional cues they pick up during interactions.

The Role of Trust in Sales

Trust is the foundation of any successful sales relationship. Without it, customers are unlikely to move forward with a purchase, no matter how great the product or service is. Trust is built through:

- **Reliability**: Delivering on promises made during the sales process.
- **Honesty**: Being transparent about the benefits and limitations of the product or service.
- **Expertise**: Demonstrating knowledge and authority in the field.
- **Consistency**: Providing a consistent experience throughout every customer interaction.

By applying psychological principles, sales professionals can build stronger, more trusting relationships with their customers, leading to higher satisfaction, repeat business, and increased referrals.

1.5 How to Apply Business Psychology to Improve Sales Performance

Now that we've explored the psychological principles behind consumer behavior, the next step is applying these insights to improve sales performance. Sales professionals can incorporate business psychology into their daily practice by:

- **Personalizing interactions**: Tailoring communication to match the emotional and psychological needs of each customer.

- **Building rapport and trust**: Using empathy, active listening, and transparency to foster strong customer relationships.

- **Leveraging psychological triggers**: Utilizing the principles of reciprocity, social proof, and scarcity to influence buying decisions.

- **Adapting based on feedback**: Continuously improving sales strategies by observing customer reactions and making adjustments based on psychological insights.

Business psychology is a powerful tool in the hands of sales professionals. By understanding the psychological factors that drive human behavior, salespeople can better influence buying decisions, build stronger customer relationships, and ultimately, increase sales success. This chapter serves as the foundation for the deeper exploration of psychological techniques and strategies that will follow in the rest of the book. By mastering these psychological insights, you'll be well on your way to transforming the way you sell.

Chapter 2
Consumer Motivation and Needs

At the core of every successful sale lies a deep understanding of consumer motivation and needs. Why do people buy certain products? What drives their purchasing decisions? The answers to these questions are often more complex than they appear on the surface. While consumers may believe they make decisions based on logic, the reality is that emotions, desires, and subconscious motivations often play a much larger role.

In this chapter, we will explore the psychological foundations of consumer motivation, examining key theories that explain why people buy what they do. We will also look at how sales professionals can identify and tap into these motivations to align their offerings with what the consumer truly needs.

2.1 What Drives Consumer Decisions?

Consumer behavior is driven by a variety of factors, including emotions, personal values, societal influences, and psychological needs. A consumer's motivation can be understood as the internal drive that pushes them to satisfy a need or want. When this need is unmet, the consumer is prompted to take action, which could include making a purchase. But motivation is not always straightforward, and it often stems from a combination of conscious and unconscious factors.

The Two Types of Motivation:

- **Intrinsic Motivation**: This is when consumers are motivated by internal factors, such as personal satisfaction, self-fulfillment, or a desire for growth. For example, a consumer might buy a self-help book because they want to improve their life.
- **Extrinsic Motivation**: This occurs when consumers are motivated by external factors, such as rewards, social recognition, or avoiding negative outcomes. For example, a consumer might buy a luxury car to gain social status or to avoid looking unsuccessful.

Most purchasing decisions involve a mix of both intrinsic and extrinsic motivations. By identifying which type of motivation is driving a customer, sales professionals can adjust their approach to better meet the customer's underlying needs.

2.2 Maslow's Hierarchy of Needs in Sales

One of the most well-known psychological frameworks for understanding human motivation is **Maslow's Hierarchy of Needs**. Developed by psychologist Abraham Maslow, this theory proposes that human needs are organized in a hierarchical order, starting with basic physiological needs and moving up to more complex emotional and psychological needs. The hierarchy consists of five levels:

1. **Physiological Needs**: Basic survival needs such as food, water, shelter, and clothing.
2. **Safety Needs**: Security, stability, and protection from harm.

3. **Love and Belonging Needs**: Emotional relationships, friendships, and social connections.

4. **Esteem Needs**: Self-esteem, respect from others, recognition, and status.

5. **Self-Actualization**: The desire to achieve one's full potential and engage in personal growth.

How Maslow's Hierarchy Applies to Sales:

Understanding where a customer falls on Maslow's hierarchy can help sales professionals tailor their pitch. For example:

- If a customer is primarily concerned with safety (level 2), they may be more interested in products that offer security, protection, or reliability (e.g., home insurance or a secure online banking service).

- A customer focused on esteem (level 4) may be drawn to luxury products or services that enhance their social status or boost their confidence (e.g., designer clothing or a high-end sports car).

- Customers who are focused on self-actualization (level 5) may be more inclined to buy products that help them achieve personal growth, such as educational courses or creative tools.

By aligning the sales message with the customer's current needs on Maslow's hierarchy, sales professionals can create a more compelling, emotionally resonant pitch.

2.3 The Psychology of Wants vs. Needs

One of the challenges in sales is differentiating between what a consumer **wants** and what they **need**. While needs are essential and often rooted in survival or personal well-being, wants are desires that can enhance comfort, happiness, or status. For example:

- **Need**: A person needs food to survive.
- **Want**: A person wants to dine at a Michelin-starred restaurant for the experience and status.

Why Consumers Buy Wants Over Needs:

Although needs are critical, consumers are often more motivated to fulfill their wants. This is because wants are tied to emotional gratification, pleasure, and a sense of fulfillment. A consumer may rationalize a purchase by saying they "need" it, but in reality, they are driven by the desire for a particular experience or emotional payoff.

How to Appeal to Wants and Needs in Sales:

- **Appealing to Needs**: Focus on how your product or service solves a problem or addresses a fundamental requirement for the customer. This is particularly effective when selling essential goods or services (e.g., health insurance, home security systems, or everyday household items).
- **Appealing to Wants**: Highlight the emotional and experiential benefits of your product or service. When selling luxury goods or non-essential products, focus on how the purchase will make the customer feel—whether that's more confident, successful, or happy.

2.4 The Role of Pain Points in Consumer Motivation

In many cases, consumer motivation stems from a desire to alleviate a **pain point**. Pain points are specific problems or frustrations that consumers are looking to solve. Sales professionals who can identify and address a customer's pain point can position their product or service as the perfect solution.

Types of Consumer Pain Points:

1. **Financial Pain Points**: Concerns about cost, value for money, or financial risk (e.g., a consumer looking to save money on monthly bills).

2. **Productivity Pain Points**: Problems related to inefficiency, wasted time, or lack of convenience (e.g., a business needing software to streamline processes).

3. **Process Pain Points**: Frustrations with complicated or time-consuming processes (e.g., a customer seeking a simpler way to make online purchases).

4. **Support Pain Points**: Concerns about customer service, reliability, or after-sales support (e.g., a consumer wanting assurance that they will receive help if something goes wrong).

How to Leverage Pain Points in Sales:

- **Identify the Pain Point**: Through active listening and asking the right questions, determine what specific problem the customer is trying to solve.

- **Offer a Solution**: Position your product or service as the ideal solution to their pain point. Focus on how it will alleviate their frustration, save them time, or reduce their costs.

- **Address Objections**: Customers may be hesitant to move forward due to concerns about price, complexity, or risk. By addressing these objections upfront and demonstrating how your offering overcomes their pain point, you can reduce resistance and increase the likelihood of closing the sale.

2.5 Tapping Into Emotional Triggers

Emotions are one of the most powerful drivers of consumer behavior. People often make purchasing decisions based on how a product or service makes them feel, rather than its logical benefits. By tapping into emotional triggers, sales professionals can create a deeper connection with the customer and drive stronger sales results.

Common Emotional Triggers in Sales:

- **Fear**: Consumers often buy products out of a desire to avoid negative outcomes, such as financial loss, physical harm, or embarrassment. For example, a home security system is sold on the fear of break-ins.

- **Desire for Pleasure**: Products that promise happiness, comfort, or excitement appeal to consumers' desire for pleasure. For example, vacations and luxury goods often tap into this emotional trigger.

- **Status and Pride**: Many consumers are motivated by the desire for social status, prestige, or recognition. Products that symbolize success or wealth—such as luxury cars or designer clothes—often play on this trigger.

- **Nostalgia**: Emotions related to fond memories of the past can be a powerful motivator. Brands that evoke a sense of nostalgia can create strong emotional connections with customers (e.g., retro products or re-released childhood favorites).

- **Belonging**: Humans have an innate need for social connection and belonging. Sales professionals can appeal to this emotion by emphasizing how their product or service will help the customer feel part of a community or group (e.g., membership-based services or products with a strong social following).

2.6 Identifying and Tapping Into Customer Needs

Identifying what motivates a customer requires active listening and a deep understanding of their unique situation. To effectively tap into consumer motivation and align your sales approach with their needs, consider the following steps:

1. Ask Open-Ended Questions

Instead of making assumptions, ask open-ended questions that encourage the customer to share more about their motivations, pain points, and desires. Questions like, "What challenges are you facing?" or "What are you hoping to achieve with this purchase?" can provide valuable insights.

2. Listen Actively

Active listening involves not just hearing the words a customer says but paying attention to their tone, body language, and emotions. This can help you pick up on underlying needs or unspoken concerns.

3. Identify Emotional Drivers

Pay attention to emotional cues, such as excitement, frustration, or fear, that may indicate what is truly motivating the customer. Once you've identified the emotional driver, you can tailor your pitch to address that need.

4. Tailor Your Approach

Once you understand the customer's needs and motivations, tailor your sales approach to match. Highlight the features and benefits of your product or service that directly address the customer's specific situation, whether that's solving a problem, fulfilling a desire, or alleviating a pain point.

Consumer motivation and needs are at the heart of the sales process. By understanding what drives consumers—whether it's the need for safety, the desire for social status, or the urge to solve a pressing problem—sales professionals can tailor their approach to better meet customer needs

Chapter 3
The Psychology of Influence and Persuasion in Sales

In the world of sales, success hinges not only on understanding consumer behavior but also on the ability to influence and persuade customers to make decisions. Influence and persuasion are powerful psychological tools that, when used ethically, can help sales professionals create compelling sales messages, build trust, and guide customers toward making favorable decisions. This chapter explores the key psychological principles of influence and persuasion, providing practical strategies to help sales professionals effectively persuade their customers.

3.1 The Science of Influence

The ability to influence others has been studied extensively in psychology, with much of the research focused on identifying the factors that lead people to say "yes" to a request. One of the most widely recognized frameworks for understanding influence comes from Dr. Robert Cialdini, a renowned psychologist who identified six key principles of influence that are particularly relevant to sales:

Cialdini's Six Principles of Influence:

1. **Reciprocity**
   - **Definition**: People feel obligated to return a favor when someone does something for them.

- **Application in Sales**: By offering something of value to your customer—such as a free sample, useful information, or a special discount—you activate the principle of reciprocity. The customer feels a subconscious urge to reciprocate, often by making a purchase or engaging further with your product.

- **Example**: A salesperson may offer a customer a free e-book or consultation. After receiving this valuable offer, the customer feels more inclined to reciprocate by moving forward with a purchase.

2. **Commitment and Consistency**

    - **Definition**: Once people commit to something, they are more likely to remain consistent with that commitment, even when the stakes are raised.

    - **Application in Sales**: Encouraging customers to make small commitments early in the sales process can lead to larger commitments later. This could be as simple as signing up for a free trial or subscribing to a newsletter. Once the customer commits to these small steps, they are more likely to make a larger purchase down the line.

    - **Example**: A customer who signs up for a free trial of a software product is more likely to purchase the full version once the trial period ends, because they have already made an initial commitment.

3. **Social Proof**

    - **Definition**: People look to the actions and behaviors of others to determine their own. Social proof is especially powerful when people are uncertain about a decision.

- **Application in Sales**: Showing customers that others have benefited from your product or service can create a sense of trust and reduce uncertainty. Testimonials, case studies, user reviews, and endorsements are effective ways to apply social proof in the sales process.
- **Example**: A website may display customer reviews and ratings prominently to demonstrate that others have had a positive experience with the product, encouraging new customers to make a purchase.

4. **Authority**
   - **Definition**: People are more likely to be influenced by someone who is perceived as an expert or authority figure in a particular field.
   - **Application in Sales**: Establishing yourself as an expert in your industry increases trust and credibility, making customers more likely to take your advice and recommendations. This can be achieved by sharing your expertise, citing your credentials, or showcasing endorsements from respected figures in the industry.
   - **Example**: A financial advisor with years of experience and relevant certifications can build authority, making it more likely that clients will trust their investment recommendations.

5. **Liking**
    - **Definition**: People are more likely to say "yes" to individuals they like and feel a personal connection with.
    - **Application in Sales**: Building rapport with customers and finding common ground can increase their likelihood of buying from you. People are naturally drawn to others who are friendly, empathetic, and share similar values or interests.
    - **Example**: A salesperson who takes the time to get to know a customer personally, finding shared hobbies or interests, can build a stronger relationship, making the customer more likely to trust their recommendations.

6. **Scarcity**
    - **Definition**: People tend to place higher value on things that are scarce or in limited supply. The fear of missing out (FOMO) is a strong motivator for many consumers.
    - **Application in Sales**: Highlighting the scarcity of a product—whether through limited-time offers, exclusive deals, or low stock levels—can create a sense of urgency, prompting customers to take action quickly.
    - **Example**: An online store might display a message such as "Only 3 items left in stock!" to encourage customers to make a purchase before the product sells out.

3.2 The Role of Trust in Persuasion

Trust is a critical factor in any persuasive interaction, especially in sales. Customers are far more likely to make a purchase when they trust the salesperson, the product, and the brand. Building trust requires a combination of transparency, authenticity, and reliability.

How to Build Trust in Sales:

1. **Be Honest and Transparent**: Be upfront about the benefits and limitations of your product. Customers appreciate honesty, and it can help prevent buyer's remorse, leading to long-term loyalty.

2. **Deliver on Promises**: Always follow through on your commitments. If you promise a quick delivery or guaranteed results, ensure that you deliver exactly what you said.

3. **Provide Social Proof**: Testimonials, case studies, and positive reviews from satisfied customers can reinforce trust and demonstrate that others have benefited from your product or service.

4. **Personalize Your Approach**: Tailor your sales message to the unique needs of each customer. Personalization shows that you care about their specific situation and are not just focused on making a sale.

5. **Demonstrate Expertise**: Position yourself as an authority in your field by sharing valuable knowledge and insights. When customers see you as an expert, they are more likely to trust your recommendations.

3.3 The Power of Emotional Appeal

Logic and facts alone are rarely enough to persuade customers to make a decision. Emotions play a significant role in the decision-making process, often guiding consumers toward a purchase even when the logical benefits of the product are unclear. Understanding how to evoke the right emotions in your customers can make the difference between a successful sale and a missed opportunity.

Common Emotional Triggers in Sales:

- **Fear**: The fear of loss or missing out can be a powerful motivator. Salespeople can leverage this by highlighting what customers stand to lose by not taking action (e.g., limited-time offers, potential risks of not solving a problem).

- **Joy**: Products that promise happiness, enjoyment, or fulfillment can tap into customers' desire for positive emotional experiences. Sales professionals can focus on how the product will make the customer feel happier or more satisfied.

- **Pride**: Consumers often buy products that enhance their self-esteem or social status. Salespeople can appeal to a customer's sense of pride by showing how the product can help them achieve recognition, success, or respect from others.

- **Guilt**: Sometimes, customers feel guilty about not addressing a need or issue (e.g., failing to invest in personal health, safety, or self-improvement). By gently reminding them of these unaddressed needs, salespeople can persuade them to take action.

How to Use Emotional Appeal in Sales:

1. **Understand the Customer's Emotional Needs**: Before making an emotional appeal, identify which emotions are most relevant to the customer's current situation. Are they motivated by fear, joy, or pride? Tailor your message accordingly.

2. **Tell Stories**: People connect emotionally with stories. Sharing a story about how your product solved a problem for someone in a similar situation can create an emotional connection and make the benefits more relatable.

3. **Use Visuals and Imagery**: Emotions are often evoked more strongly through visual stimuli than through words alone. Use images, videos, or demonstrations that highlight the emotional benefits of your product or service.

4. **Create a Sense of Urgency**: Emotions like fear of missing out can be amplified by creating a sense of urgency. Limited-time offers, exclusive deals, and countdown timers can evoke an emotional response and prompt immediate action.

3.4 Overcoming Objections with Persuasion Techniques

No matter how persuasive your pitch, customers will often raise objections. These objections can range from concerns about price to doubts about the product's effectiveness. Successful sales professionals know how to address these objections using persuasive techniques that reassure the customer and guide them toward making a purchase.

Common Objections in Sales and How to Overcome Them:

1. **Price Objections**:
   - **The Objection**: "It's too expensive" or "I can't afford it."
   - **Persuasion Technique**: Highlight the value of the product rather than focusing solely on the price. Explain how the long-term benefits or cost savings outweigh the initial investment. You can also break down the cost into smaller payments (e.g., "It's just $2 per day").

2. **Product Objections**:
   - **The Objection**: "I'm not sure this product will work for me."
   - **Persuasion Technique**: Provide evidence in the form of case studies, testimonials, or guarantees that demonstrate the product's effectiveness. Offer a trial period or money-back guarantee to reduce the perceived risk.

3. **Timing Objections**:
   - **The Objection**: "I'm not ready to make a decision right now."
   - **Persuasion Technique**: Create a sense of urgency by highlighting limited-time offers or the consequences of waiting too long. Use scarcity to show that the opportunity might not be available in the future.

4. **Trust Objections**:
   - **The Objection**: "I don't trust this company" or "I'm worried about the quality."
   - **Persuasion Technique**: Build trust by sharing success stories, certifications, and customer reviews. Offer transparency in your processes and a clear return policy to give the customer peace of mind.

3.5 Ethical Persuasion in Sales

While the principles of influence and persuasion can be incredibly powerful, it's important for sales professionals to use them ethically. Manipulating or deceiving customers into making a purchase can lead to long-term damage to your reputation and customer relationships. Ethical persuasion is about guiding customers toward decisions that are in their best interest, while maintaining transparency and integrity.

Guidelines for Ethical Persuasion:

- **Be Honest**: Never make false claims or exaggerate the benefits of your product. Ensure that your sales message is truthful and accurate.
- **Respect the Customer's Autonomy**: Persuasion should never feel coercive. Allow customers the freedom to make their own decisions and respect their right to say no.
- **Focus on Value**: Always strive to provide genuine value to your customers. Ethical persuasion is about helping customers find solutions that truly meet their needs, not just closing a sale at any cost.

- **Be Transparent**: Make sure customers understand the full terms of the sale, including any potential risks or limitations. Avoid hiding important details that could affect their decision.

The psychology of influence and persuasion is a powerful tool in sales. By understanding the key principles of influence, building trust, appealing to emotions, and overcoming objections, sales professionals can create compelling sales strategies that resonate with their customers. When used ethically, these techniques not only increase sales but also build long-term, trusting relationships with customers.

Chapter 4
The Role of Personality in Sales Success

Personality plays a pivotal role in sales. Both the personality of the salesperson and that of the customer can significantly influence the sales process and its outcome. Understanding different personality types, knowing how to adapt to them, and leveraging your own strengths can increase your ability to connect with clients, build rapport, and close deals. In this chapter, we explore how personality affects sales, the various personality frameworks used to understand behavior, and how sales professionals can adjust their approach to suit different customers.

4.1 Why Personality Matters in Sales

Sales is a relationship-driven profession, and relationships are deeply influenced by personality. People naturally connect with those who resonate with their own temperament, communication style, and preferences. A sales professional who understands and adapts to the personality of their client is far more likely to create rapport, reduce resistance, and build trust.

Key Ways Personality Affects Sales Success:

1. **Communication Style**: Different personality types prefer different ways of communicating. Some clients prefer detailed, fact-based discussions, while others

respond better to casual, relationship-focused conversations. Tailoring your communication style to the personality of the customer makes the sales interaction smoother and more effective.

2. **Decision-Making Process**: Personality also influences how quickly and confidently people make decisions. Some individuals are more analytical and need time to process information, while others are impulsive and can make decisions on the spot. Understanding this helps in managing expectations and timing your approach.

3. **Conflict Resolution**: Handling objections, questions, or concerns is an essential part of the sales process. Personality plays a role in how both the salesperson and the customer approach and resolve conflict. Some customers may be more confrontational, while others may avoid conflict altogether. Sales professionals must learn to navigate these different dynamics effectively.

4.2 Personality Models in Sales

Several psychological frameworks can help sales professionals better understand the different personality types they encounter in their work. The two most commonly used in sales are the **DISC model** and the **Big Five Personality Traits**. These models categorize behavior patterns that can be useful in tailoring sales strategies to different individuals.

The DISC Model of Personality

The **DISC** model, developed by psychologist William Marston, categorizes people into four main personality types based on their behaviors and preferences. Each type responds to different sales approaches, making DISC a useful tool for sales professionals.

1. **Dominance (D)**
   - **Characteristics**: Goal-oriented, direct, competitive, decisive, and assertive. People with this personality type prefer to be in control and dislike being micromanaged.
   - **How to Sell to Them**: Be direct and to the point. Focus on results and how your product can help them achieve their goals. Avoid unnecessary details and give them options that allow them to feel in control.

2. **Influence (I)**
   - **Characteristics**: Outgoing, enthusiastic, social, and persuasive. These individuals are driven by social connections and enjoy engaging with others.
   - **How to Sell to Them**: Build a personal connection and engage them in a lively conversation. Focus on the social or emotional benefits of your product and how it can improve their lifestyle. They respond well to positive energy and enthusiasm.

3. **Steadiness (S)**
   - **Characteristics**: Patient, calm, loyal, and cooperative. They value stability, consistency, and long-term relationships.
   - **How to Sell to Them**: Be patient and build trust. Steadiness types appreciate a slower-paced, relationship-driven sales process where they don't feel pressured. Focus on reliability and long-term benefits.

4. **Conscientiousness (C)**
    - **Characteristics**: Analytical, detail-oriented, methodical, and cautious. They prefer to make decisions based on facts, data, and logic.
    - **How to Sell to Them**: Provide detailed information and be prepared to answer questions thoroughly. Avoid overly emotional appeals and instead focus on the practical, logical benefits of your product. Be accurate and precise in your responses.

The Big Five Personality Traits

The **Big Five Personality Traits**, also known as the **OCEAN model,** is another popular psychological framework. It classifies individuals based on five core dimensions:

1. **Openness to Experience**: Creativity, curiosity, and a willingness to try new things.
    - **How to Sell to High Openness**: Emphasize innovation, newness, and possibilities. These customers are likely to be interested in unique or cutting-edge products.
2. **Conscientiousness**: Organization, dependability, and attention to detail.
    - **How to Sell to High Conscientiousness**: Focus on reliability, precision, and well-documented information. They value careful consideration and consistency.

3. **Extraversion**: Sociability, assertiveness, and talkativeness.
   - **How to Sell to High Extraversion**: Engage them in energetic conversations and emphasize social benefits. These clients often appreciate charisma and a lively interaction.
4. **Agreeableness**: Compassion, cooperation, and friendliness.
   - **How to Sell to High Agreeableness**: Focus on building rapport and trust. They respond well to empathy and a sales approach that highlights how the product helps others or improves harmony.
5. **Neuroticism**: Emotional stability and tendency toward anxiety or negativity.
   - **How to Sell to High Neuroticism**: Address concerns and offer reassurance. People higher in neuroticism may need more time to feel comfortable with a decision, and they'll appreciate a calm, patient approach that reduces their anxieties.

4.3 Adapting Sales Approaches to Different Personality Types

Sales professionals who can adapt their approach based on the personality of the customer stand a much better chance of success. This involves recognizing personality traits quickly and adjusting communication style, pace, and the structure of the sales pitch to match the client's preferences.

Steps for Adapting Your Sales Strategy:

1. **Identify the Customer's Personality Type**: Early in the conversation, look for clues about the customer's communication style, decision-making process, and emotional tone. Are they asking for a lot of details (Conscientious)? Are they focused on social proof and enthusiastic engagement (Influence)? This can help you categorize their personality type quickly.

2. **Adjust Communication Style**: Once you have identified the personality type, adapt your communication to suit their preferences. For example, be direct and assertive with Dominance types, while using a more friendly, conversational approach with Influence types.

3. **Pace the Conversation Appropriately**: Different personality types prefer different speeds. Dominance types want quick, efficient conversations, while Steadiness types prefer to take their time. Match your pacing to the customer's comfort level.

4. **Tailor Your Value Proposition**: Emphasize different aspects of your product depending on the personality of the customer. Analytical types (Conscientious) will appreciate data and performance metrics, while social types (Influence) will respond to the emotional and social impact of the product.

5. **Handle Objections Differently**: Each personality type will respond differently to objections or concerns. A Dominance type may want a straightforward, no-nonsense rebuttal, while a Steadiness type will

appreciate a more empathetic, relationship-driven approach.

4.4 The Salesperson's Personality and Its Impact on Sales

Just as the customer's personality matters, the personality of the salesperson also influences the sales process. A self-aware salesperson can leverage their strengths and address any weaknesses to improve their performance.

Common Salesperson Personality Types and Their Strengths:

1. **The Charismatic Salesperson**: Outgoing, energetic, and persuasive. These salespeople are often skilled at building rapport quickly and generating excitement about a product.
    - **Strengths**: Great at engaging clients, creating enthusiasm, and closing deals quickly.
    - **Challenges**: May overlook detail-oriented clients who need more information or time to decide.

2. **The Analytical Salesperson**: Methodical, detail-oriented, and knowledgeable. These salespeople excel in providing data, facts, and well-reasoned arguments.
    - **Strengths**: Ideal for selling to clients who value precision and detail.
    - **Challenges**: May struggle to engage more emotional, impulsive buyers who respond better to enthusiasm and relationship-building.

3. **The Empathetic Salesperson**: Compassionate, patient, and focused on building relationships. These

salespeople excel at creating long-term client relationships based on trust.

- **Strengths**: Excellent at handling difficult customers and building loyalty.
- **Challenges**: May be too cautious or conflict-averse when closing deals, leading to missed opportunities.

4. **The Assertive Salesperson**: Confident, goal-driven, and focused on results. These salespeople are often highly competitive and determined to meet or exceed their targets.

    - **Strengths**: Great at closing deals and pushing customers to make decisions.
    - **Challenges**: Can be too aggressive for certain personality types, leading to resistance or lost sales.

How Sales Professionals Can Leverage Their Strengths:

1. **Self-Awareness**: Understand your natural strengths and tendencies as a salesperson. Are you more analytical, empathetic, or assertive? Knowing this allows you to capitalize on your strengths and be mindful of areas where you might need to adapt.
2. **Continuous Improvement**: Even the most successful salespeople can benefit from improving their weaker areas. For example, an assertive salesperson might work on developing more empathy, while an empathetic salesperson could work on being more assertive in closing deals.

3. **Personal Branding**: Embrace your personality and use it to your advantage. Clients appreciate authenticity, and being true to yourself can help build trust. If you are naturally enthusiastic, let that shine in your interactions.

4.5 Personality Conflicts in Sales

Not all personality types will naturally mesh. Sometimes, the salesperson's personality may clash with the customer's, making it difficult to build rapport or move the sales process forward. Recognizing these conflicts early and taking steps to mitigate them can save the sale.

How to Navigate Personality Conflicts:

1. **Recognize the Conflict**: Pay attention to signs of discomfort or misalignment, such as a customer becoming distant, resistant, or disengaged.
2. **Adapt and Adjust**: If you sense that your natural style is not resonating with the customer, adjust your approach. For example, if you're highly energetic and the customer seems overwhelmed, slow down and focus on a more measured, calm conversation.
3. **Bring in a Team Member**: In some cases, you may benefit from bringing in another team member who has a personality type that better matches the client. Team selling can help resolve personality clashes and improve the chances of closing the deal.

Personality is a powerful factor in sales. By understanding both your own personality and that of your customers, you can tailor your approach to create better connections, build trust, and ultimately increase your success rate. Whether you're using frameworks like DISC or the Big Five to analyze behavior or simply learning to adapt to different communication styles, mastering the art of personality-driven selling can significantly enhance your effectiveness as a sales professional.

Chapter 5
Emotional Intelligence in Sales

In today's competitive business environment, emotional intelligence (EI) has become a key differentiator for successful sales professionals. While product knowledge, strategy, and communication skills are critical components of sales success, emotional intelligence adds an extra dimension that allows salespeople to connect with their clients on a deeper level, understand their needs, and navigate complex emotional dynamics. This chapter explores the role of emotional intelligence in sales, its key components, and practical strategies for developing and leveraging EI to build stronger relationships and improve sales outcomes.

5.1 Understanding Emotional Intelligence (EI)

Emotional intelligence refers to the ability to recognize, understand, and manage your own emotions, as well as the emotions of others. In a sales context, this means being able to read your clients' emotional states, respond appropriately, and adjust your approach to align with their emotional needs and expectations.

The Four Key Components of Emotional Intelligence:

1. **Self-Awareness**: The ability to recognize and understand your own emotions, as well as how they affect your thoughts and behavior. Salespeople with high self-awareness are mindful of their emotional

triggers, enabling them to remain calm and composed during high-pressure situations.

2. **Self-Management**: This refers to the ability to control and regulate your emotions, especially in stressful or challenging situations. Effective self-management allows sales professionals to stay positive, resilient, and focused even when facing rejection or difficult clients.

3. **Social Awareness**: Also known as empathy, social awareness is the ability to understand the emotions of others and pick up on social cues. In sales, this involves being attuned to the customer's feelings, needs, and concerns, and responding in a way that fosters trust and rapport.

4. **Relationship Management**: This is the ability to use emotional awareness to build and manage relationships effectively. In sales, relationship management involves conflict resolution, negotiation, and collaboration to ensure long-term customer satisfaction and loyalty.

5.2 The Importance of Emotional Intelligence in Sales

Sales is not just about transactions—it's about relationships. Emotional intelligence plays a critical role in fostering these relationships, as it allows sales professionals to connect with customers on a personal level, respond to their emotional needs, and create a positive, lasting impression.

How EI Impacts Sales Success:

1. **Building Rapport**: Customers are more likely to buy from people they trust and feel comfortable with. Emotionally intelligent salespeople can build rapport quickly by showing empathy, being attentive to the

customer's concerns, and adjusting their communication style to suit the customer's emotional state.

2. **Understanding Customer Needs**: Emotional intelligence helps sales professionals go beyond surface-level needs to understand the deeper, emotional drivers behind a customer's buying decisions. By recognizing the customer's emotional triggers, salespeople can tailor their pitch to appeal to these underlying motivations.

3. **Managing Rejection and Objections**: Sales professionals encounter rejection regularly, which can be emotionally challenging. Those with high emotional intelligence can manage these emotions effectively, allowing them to stay positive and maintain their confidence. They are also better equipped to handle objections with empathy and understanding, rather than becoming defensive or discouraged.

4. **Closing Deals**: Emotionally intelligent salespeople know how to read a customer's emotional readiness to close a deal. They can sense when a customer is feeling uncertain, excited, or hesitant and adjust their approach to either provide reassurance or seize the moment to finalize the sale.

5. **Long-Term Customer Relationships**: Customers appreciate salespeople who understand their needs, respect their emotions, and build genuine connections. Emotional intelligence fosters loyalty by ensuring that customers feel valued, understood, and supported throughout the sales process.

5.3 Developing Emotional Intelligence in Sales

While some individuals may naturally possess a high level of emotional intelligence, it's a skill that can be developed and strengthened over time. Sales professionals can cultivate their EI through self-awareness exercises, active listening, empathy-building techniques, and emotional regulation strategies.

Strategies for Developing Emotional Intelligence:

1. **Practice Self-Awareness**:
    - **Reflect on Your Emotions**: Take time to reflect on your emotions after a sales interaction. How did you feel during the meeting? Did certain emotions affect your performance? By regularly assessing your emotional responses, you can become more attuned to your emotional triggers.
    - **Keep a Journal**: Keeping a journal to track your emotional reactions to different sales situations can help you identify patterns and areas for improvement.
2. **Improve Self-Management**:
    - **Develop Stress-Management Techniques**: Sales can be stressful, so it's important to develop techniques for managing your emotions in high-pressure situations. Techniques such as deep breathing, mindfulness, and positive visualization can help you stay calm and focused.
    - **Delay Immediate Reactions**: When faced with a difficult situation or emotional trigger, give yourself time to process your emotions before

responding. This prevents emotional outbursts and helps you maintain professionalism.

3. **Enhance Social Awareness**:
    - **Practice Active Listening**: Listening is one of the most important skills in emotional intelligence. Focus on truly understanding your customer's words, tone, and body language. Avoid interrupting and show genuine interest in what they are saying.
    - **Read Emotional Cues**: Pay attention to your customer's non-verbal communication, such as facial expressions, posture, and tone of voice. These cues can provide valuable insight into how they are feeling and what they need from you at that moment.

4. **Strengthen Relationship Management**:
    - **Show Empathy**: Empathy is the foundation of emotional intelligence. Put yourself in your customer's shoes and try to understand their perspective. Even if you don't agree with them, showing empathy can help build trust and rapport.
    - **Be Proactive in Conflict Resolution**: Don't shy away from addressing conflicts or disagreements with customers. Approach conflicts with a calm and solution-focused mindset, aiming to resolve issues in a way that benefits both parties.

5.4 Emotional Intelligence in Handling Difficult Customers

Dealing with difficult customers is an inevitable part of sales. Whether a client is frustrated, indecisive, or uncooperative, emotional intelligence can help you navigate these interactions more effectively.

Common Types of Difficult Customers:

1. **The Angry Customer**: These customers may express frustration or anger due to a previous negative experience or unmet expectations. Without emotional intelligence, a salesperson might react defensively, which could escalate the situation.

    o **EI Approach**: Stay calm and listen actively. Acknowledge their emotions and validate their concerns. Use empathy to diffuse their anger and offer solutions to resolve the issue.

2. **The Indecisive Customer**: Some customers struggle to make decisions, often second-guessing their choices or requesting more information repeatedly. This can be frustrating for salespeople who are eager to close the deal.

    o **EI Approach**: Use patience and reassurance. Ask open-ended questions to understand their hesitations and provide clear, concise information to help them feel more confident in their decision.

3. **The Demanding Customer**: These customers may have high expectations, frequently asking for discounts, special treatment, or immediate solutions. Their behavior can come across as entitled or unreasonable.

    o **EI Approach**: Set boundaries respectfully. While it's important to meet customer needs, it's also crucial to manage expectations. Stay assertive but empathetic, explaining what is feasible without compromising the relationship.

4. **The Silent Customer**: Some customers are difficult because they provide very little feedback or input. This makes it challenging for the salesperson to gauge their interest or address their concerns.
    - **EI Approach**: Encourage open communication by asking specific, non-confrontational questions. Use emotional intelligence to read their non-verbal cues and gently guide the conversation toward their needs and preferences.

5.5 Emotional Triggers in Sales

Emotions often drive buying decisions more than logic. Emotional triggers are psychological cues that influence a customer's feelings and can significantly impact their purchasing behavior. By identifying and appealing to these emotional triggers, sales professionals can create more compelling and persuasive sales experiences.

Common Emotional Triggers in Sales:

1. **Fear of Missing Out (FOMO)**: Customers often fear that they will miss out on a valuable opportunity, which can drive them to make a purchase.
    - **Sales Strategy**: Use limited-time offers, exclusive deals, or product scarcity to tap into this emotional trigger.
2. **Desire for Status**: Many customers are motivated by the desire to enhance their status or self-image through their purchases.
    - **Sales Strategy**: Highlight how your product can improve the customer's lifestyle, reputation, or social standing.

3. **Security and Comfort**: Some customers are driven by a need for security, whether financial, physical, or emotional. Products that offer peace of mind, protection, or convenience can appeal to this trigger.
    - **Sales Strategy**: Emphasize the reliability, safety, and long-term benefits of your product.
4. **Pleasure and Happiness**: Customers often seek products that will bring them joy, satisfaction, or fulfillment.
    - **Sales Strategy**: Focus on how your product enhances the customer's quality of life or delivers an enjoyable experience.

Emotional intelligence is a critical skill for sales professionals, enabling them to connect with customers on a deeper level, manage complex emotional dynamics, and navigate challenging sales situations with confidence. By developing self-awareness, self-management, social awareness, and relationship management skills, salespeople can create meaningful, long-lasting relationships with their customers, resulting in increased loyalty and sales success. Moreover, leveraging emotional triggers ethically and understanding the emotional landscape of your customers will enhance your ability to influence purchasing decisions and close deals more effectively.

Chapter 6

Building Rapport and Trust in Sales

Establishing rapport and trust is essential in sales, as these elements form the foundation of successful client relationships. Customers are more likely to make purchases and continue doing business with sales professionals they trust. This chapter explores the importance of building rapport and trust in sales, techniques for creating genuine connections with customers, and strategies for maintaining these relationships over time.

6.1 The Importance of Rapport and Trust in Sales

Rapport refers to a harmonious relationship characterized by mutual understanding, respect, and empathy. Trust, on the other hand, is the belief that a salesperson is reliable, competent, and acts in the customer's best interest. Both rapport and trust are crucial for the following reasons:

Benefits of Building Rapport and Trust:

1. **Increased Sales Opportunities**: Customers are more likely to buy from someone they feel comfortable with. A strong rapport increases the likelihood of repeat business and referrals, leading to more sales opportunities.

2. **Enhanced Customer Loyalty**: Trust fosters loyalty. When customers feel a connection with a salesperson,

they are more likely to return for future purchases and recommend the salesperson to others.

3. **Reduced Resistance**: Building rapport can minimize objections and resistance during the sales process. Customers are more receptive to proposals from salespeople they trust and feel connected to.

4. **Better Understanding of Customer Needs**: Establishing rapport allows sales professionals to gain deeper insights into the customer's needs, preferences, and pain points, enabling them to tailor their solutions more effectively.

5. **Smoother Negotiations**: When trust exists, negotiations become less contentious. Customers are more likely to be open about their concerns and work collaboratively toward a solution that benefits both parties.

6.2 Techniques for Building Rapport

Building rapport with customers involves creating a positive, genuine connection. Here are some effective techniques to foster rapport during sales interactions:

1. Active Listening:

Active listening involves fully focusing on what the customer is saying, rather than merely waiting for your turn to speak. This technique demonstrates respect and empathy, which are essential for rapport building.

- **Tips for Active Listening**:
    o Make eye contact and nod to show understanding.

- Paraphrase what the customer says to confirm comprehension.
- Avoid interrupting and allow them to express their thoughts fully.

2. Find Common Ground:

Discovering shared interests or experiences can help establish a connection with the customer. This common ground can be anything from personal interests, professional backgrounds, or mutual acquaintances.

- **Tips for Finding Common Ground**:
    - Research the customer before the meeting to learn about their interests or background.
    - Share a personal anecdote that relates to the customer's experiences, creating a relatable context.

3. Use Empathy:

Empathy involves understanding and validating the customer's feelings and perspectives. Demonstrating empathy shows that you care about their needs and concerns, which is crucial for building trust.

- **Tips for Practicing Empathy**:
    - Acknowledge the customer's emotions. For instance, if they express frustration, validate their feelings by saying, "I understand how that can be frustrating."
    - Ask open-ended questions to encourage customers to share more about their experiences and feelings.

4. Personalize Interactions:

Treating customers as individuals rather than transactions fosters a sense of connection. Personalizing interactions can create a more meaningful relationship.

- **Tips for Personalization**:
    - Use the customer's name frequently during the conversation to create a sense of familiarity.
    - Tailor your communication style to match the customer's preferences, whether they prefer formal or informal interactions.

5. Show Authenticity:

Being genuine and authentic is vital for building trust. Customers can often sense insincerity, which can undermine rapport.

- **Tips for Showing Authenticity**:
    - Be transparent about your intentions and product offerings.
    - Share your own experiences and challenges, making you relatable and trustworthy.

6.3 Strategies for Establishing Trust

While rapport is about creating a connection, trust is built over time through consistent actions and behaviors. Here are key strategies for establishing and maintaining trust with customers:

1. Be Honest and Transparent:

Honesty is the cornerstone of trust. Always provide accurate information, even if it means acknowledging limitations or weaknesses in your product.

- **Tips for Honesty and Transparency**:
    - Avoid making exaggerated claims or promises that you cannot fulfill.
    - If a customer has a specific need that your product doesn't meet, be upfront about it and suggest alternatives.

2. Deliver on Promises:

Consistency is critical in building trust. Follow through on commitments, whether they are related to product delivery, service levels, or follow-up communications.

- **Tips for Delivering on Promises**:
    - Set realistic expectations and ensure you can meet them before making commitments.
    - If unexpected delays occur, communicate proactively with the customer to keep them informed.

3. Provide Value Before Selling:

Offering valuable insights, resources, or support before making a sale can help establish you as a trusted advisor rather than just a salesperson.

- **Tips for Providing Value**:
    - Share relevant articles, case studies, or market trends that may benefit the customer.

- Offer free consultations or assessments to showcase your expertise and commitment to their success.

4. Foster Open Communication:

Encouraging open communication builds trust by allowing customers to express their thoughts, concerns, and feedback freely.

- **Tips for Encouraging Communication**:
    - Create a safe space for customers to voice their concerns without fear of judgment.
    - Regularly check in with customers, even after a sale, to ensure their satisfaction and address any issues that may arise.

5. Be Responsive and Accessible:

Being available and responsive to customer inquiries and concerns demonstrates that you value their business and are committed to providing excellent service.

- **Tips for Responsiveness**:
    - Set up clear communication channels and respond to inquiries promptly.
    - Use technology, such as CRM systems, to track interactions and ensure timely follow-ups.

6.4 Maintaining Rapport and Trust Over Time

Building rapport and trust is not a one-time effort; it requires ongoing attention and nurturing. Here are some strategies for maintaining strong relationships with customers:

1. Regular Check-Ins:

Schedule periodic check-ins with customers to maintain the relationship and show that you care about their ongoing needs.

- **Tips for Check-Ins**:
    - Use email, phone calls, or in-person visits to touch base.
    - Ask about their satisfaction with your product and any changes in their needs or challenges.

2. Solicit Feedback:

Encouraging and acting on customer feedback demonstrates that you value their opinions and are committed to improvement.

- **Tips for Soliciting Feedback**:
    - Use surveys, interviews, or informal conversations to gather insights on their experience.
    - Implement changes based on feedback to show customers that their voices are heard.

3. Celebrate Milestones:

Acknowledging important milestones, such as anniversaries or achievements, can reinforce the relationship and make customers feel valued.

- **Tips for Celebrating Milestones**:
    - Send personalized messages or small tokens of appreciation to commemorate special occasions.

- Recognize their successes in your communications, reinforcing a sense of partnership.

4. Stay Engaged:

Maintain engagement with customers through relevant content, updates, and resources that align with their interests.

- **Tips for Staying Engaged**:
    - Share industry news, trends, or tips through newsletters or social media.
    - Invite customers to webinars, workshops, or events that align with their interests.

5. Build a Community:

Fostering a sense of community among your customers can enhance relationships and create a network of support.

- **Tips for Building Community**:
    - Create forums, online groups, or user communities where customers can connect and share experiences.
    - Encourage customers to share success stories and tips with one another.

Building rapport and trust is an essential aspect of the sales process that significantly influences a salesperson's success. By employing techniques to establish genuine connections and strategies to maintain trust over time, sales professionals can create lasting relationships with their clients. These relationships lead to increased sales, enhanced customer loyalty, and a more fulfilling sales experience. Ultimately, rapport and trust are not just about closing deals; they are about fostering partnerships that drive mutual success. In the competitive world of sales, the ability to connect with customers on a human level will set you apart and ensure long-term success.

Chapter 7
Effective Communication Skills in Sales

Effective communication is the cornerstone of successful sales interactions. It encompasses not only the words spoken but also body language, tone, and active listening. In sales, the ability to convey information clearly, build rapport, and respond to customer needs is crucial for closing deals and fostering long-term relationships. This chapter delves into the essential communication skills required in sales, strategies for improving these skills, and the importance of adapting communication styles to different customers.

7.1 The Role of Communication in Sales

Communication in sales serves several key purposes, including informing, persuading, and building relationships. It plays a vital role in every stage of the sales process, from initial contact to closing the deal and beyond. Here are some of the key functions of communication in sales:

Functions of Communication in Sales:

1. **Information Sharing**: Sales professionals must clearly convey product features, benefits, and value propositions to customers. This requires the ability to break down complex information into easily digestible segments.

2. **Building Rapport**: Effective communication helps establish a connection with customers. By using open-ended questions and active listening, salespeople can create a comfortable atmosphere that encourages customers to share their needs and concerns.

3. **Persuasion**: Sales is inherently persuasive. The ability to articulate how a product meets a customer's specific needs is essential for convincing them to make a purchase.

4. **Problem Solving**: Customers often approach salespeople with challenges or issues. Effective communication enables sales professionals to understand these problems and provide tailored solutions.

5. **Feedback Gathering**: Communication is a two-way street. Gathering feedback from customers helps sales professionals understand their experiences and make necessary adjustments to improve service.

7.2 Key Communication Skills for Sales

Successful sales professionals possess a variety of communication skills that enable them to engage effectively with customers. Here are some of the most important skills:

1. Active Listening:

Active listening involves fully concentrating on what the speaker is saying and responding thoughtfully. It shows customers that their opinions are valued and fosters trust.

- **How to Practice Active Listening**:
    - Maintain eye contact and nod to show understanding.

- Avoid interrupting the speaker and allow them to finish their thoughts.
- Summarize or paraphrase what the customer has said to confirm your understanding.

2. Clarity and Conciseness:

Effective communication requires clarity and conciseness. Sales professionals must be able to convey complex information in simple terms, ensuring customers understand the benefits of the product.

- **Tips for Being Clear and Concise**:
    - Use straightforward language and avoid jargon unless you are sure the customer understands it.
    - Focus on the key points and avoid unnecessary details that may confuse the customer.

3. Empathy:

Empathy is the ability to understand and share the feelings of others. In sales, empathetic communication helps build rapport and demonstrates a genuine interest in the customer's needs.

- **How to Demonstrate Empathy**:
    - Acknowledge the customer's emotions and concerns. For example, if a customer expresses frustration, validate their feelings by saying, "I can understand why that would be frustrating."
    - Use phrases that reflect empathy, such as "I see where you're coming from" or "That sounds challenging."

4. Non-Verbal Communication:

Non-verbal cues, such as body language, facial expressions, and tone of voice, play a significant role in how messages are received. Effective sales professionals are aware of their own non-verbal signals and those of their customers.

- **Tips for Improving Non-Verbal Communication**:
    - Maintain an open posture and avoid crossing your arms, which can signal defensiveness.
    - Use facial expressions that match your message; a smile can convey friendliness and approachability.
    - Pay attention to your tone of voice. A warm, friendly tone can enhance your message and make you more relatable.

5. Persuasive Communication:

Sales professionals must be able to persuade customers by effectively articulating the value of their product or service. This requires a deep understanding of the customer's needs and how the product meets those needs.

- **Strategies for Persuasive Communication**:
    - Use storytelling to illustrate how the product has helped others. Stories can create an emotional connection and make the benefits more relatable.
    - Highlight key benefits and outcomes rather than just features. Explain how the product will solve the customer's problems or improve their situation.

7.3 Adapting Communication Styles

Every customer is unique, and effective sales communication involves adapting your style to match the preferences of different customers. Understanding different communication styles can help you engage more effectively.

1. Identifying Communication Styles:

Common communication styles include:

- **Direct Communicators**: These individuals value straightforwardness and efficiency. They appreciate clear, concise information and may become frustrated with lengthy explanations.

- **Analytical Communicators**: These customers seek detailed information and data. They prefer in-depth discussions and may ask many questions to fully understand the product.

- **Relational Communicators**: These individuals prioritize personal connections and may focus on building relationships over specific details. They appreciate empathy and rapport-building.

- **Expressive Communicators**: These customers are often enthusiastic and value creativity and emotional appeal. They respond well to stories and persuasive language.

2. Adapting Your Style:

Once you've identified the customer's communication style, adapt your approach accordingly:

- **For Direct Communicators**: Be straightforward and get to the point quickly. Provide essential information without unnecessary elaboration.

- **For Analytical Communicators**: Offer detailed information, statistics, and case studies. Be prepared to answer questions and provide evidence to support your claims.

- **For Relational Communicators**: Focus on building rapport. Share personal anecdotes, ask about their experiences, and engage in friendly conversation.

- **For Expressive Communicators**: Use storytelling and persuasive language. Appeal to their emotions and highlight the positive outcomes of using your product.

7.4 Handling Difficult Conversations

Difficult conversations are inevitable in sales. Whether it's addressing a complaint, handling objections, or negotiating terms, effective communication skills are essential for navigating these situations successfully.

1. Addressing Complaints:

When customers express dissatisfaction, it's crucial to handle their complaints with care and professionalism.

- **Tips for Addressing Complaints**:
    - Listen actively to the customer's concerns without interrupting.
    - Acknowledge their feelings and express empathy for their situation.
    - Offer a solution or alternative and follow up to ensure their satisfaction.

2. Handling Objections:

Objections are a natural part of the sales process. How you respond can significantly impact the customer's perception of you and your product.

- **Tips for Handling Objections**:
    - Anticipate common objections and prepare thoughtful responses in advance.
    - Use open-ended questions to understand the root of the objection better.
    - Respond with empathy and provide solutions that address the customer's concerns.

3. Negotiating Terms:

Negotiations require effective communication to ensure both parties feel satisfied with the outcome.

- **Tips for Successful Negotiation**:
    - Establish common ground and show willingness to collaborate.
    - Use clear, direct language when discussing terms and conditions.
    - Maintain a positive tone and focus on win-win solutions.

Effective communication is a fundamental skill for sales professionals. By mastering active listening, clarity, empathy, non-verbal cues, and persuasive techniques, salespeople can engage customers meaningfully and foster strong relationships. Adapting communication styles to meet the needs of different customers and handling difficult conversations with confidence further enhances the ability to connect with clients and close sales. Ultimately, effective communication not only drives sales success but also builds lasting partnerships that benefit both the salesperson and the customer. In a world where authentic connections are increasingly valued, honing your communication skills is essential for achieving long-term success in sales.

Chapter 8
Understanding Customer Behavior and Decision-Making

Understanding customer behavior and the decision-making process is crucial for effective sales strategies. Customers' purchasing decisions are influenced by a variety of psychological, social, and emotional factors. In this chapter, we will explore the different aspects of customer behavior, the stages of the decision-making process, and how sales professionals can leverage this knowledge to enhance their selling techniques.

8.1 The Importance of Understanding Customer Behavior

Understanding customer behavior enables sales professionals to tailor their approaches and improve their effectiveness. Insights into why customers make certain choices can lead to better-targeted strategies and ultimately higher conversion rates.

Key Benefits of Understanding Customer Behavior:

1. **Enhanced Targeting**: By understanding customer motivations and preferences, sales professionals can identify and target the right audience more effectively.

2. **Improved Customer Experience**: Insight into customer behavior helps in crafting personalized experiences that resonate with individual needs, leading to increased satisfaction and loyalty.

3. **Anticipating Needs**: Understanding how customers think and behave allows sales professionals to anticipate needs and present solutions before the customer even realizes they have a problem.

4. **Informed Sales Strategies**: Knowledge of customer behavior can inform marketing campaigns, sales pitches, and product development, ensuring alignment with customer expectations.

8.2 Factors Influencing Customer Behavior

Several factors influence customer behavior, including psychological, social, and cultural aspects. Understanding these factors can help sales professionals better connect with customers.

1. Psychological Factors:

These factors encompass individual motivations, perceptions, beliefs, and attitudes that influence purchasing decisions:

- **Motivation**: Understanding what motivates customers to buy is crucial. Motivation can be driven by needs (Maslow's hierarchy), desires for status, or the pursuit of solutions to specific problems.

- **Perception**: How customers perceive a product or brand significantly impacts their decision-making. Sales professionals should focus on shaping positive perceptions through branding and marketing.

- **Beliefs and Attitudes**: Customer beliefs and attitudes toward a product or service can be shaped by prior experiences, advertising, and social influences.

Understanding these beliefs can help in addressing objections and concerns.

2. Social Factors:

Customers are influenced by their social environment, including family, friends, and societal norms:

- **Reference Groups**: People often look to family, friends, or peer groups for guidance on purchasing decisions. Understanding these reference groups can help sales professionals identify influencers.

- **Social Status**: Customers may make purchasing decisions based on social status or the desire to fit in with a particular group. Sales professionals can appeal to this need by emphasizing status-related benefits.

- **Cultural Influences**: Culture shapes values, beliefs, and behaviors. Sales strategies should take cultural differences into account to ensure resonance with diverse customer bases.

3. Emotional Factors:

Emotions play a significant role in decision-making. Customers often rely on their feelings when making purchases:

- **Emotional Triggers**: Understanding what emotional triggers influence customers can help sales professionals craft compelling messages. For instance, storytelling can evoke emotions and connect customers to a brand.

- **Fear and Security**: Customers may be motivated by fear of missing out (FOMO) or the desire for security. Highlighting features that address these concerns can be effective.

8.3 The Customer Decision-Making Process

Customers typically go through several stages when making purchasing decisions. Understanding these stages allows sales professionals to engage effectively at each point.

1. Problem Recognition:

The decision-making process begins when a customer recognizes a need or problem. This can be triggered by internal stimuli (e.g., hunger) or external stimuli (e.g., advertising).

- **Sales Implication**: Sales professionals should be adept at identifying potential needs and presenting solutions that resonate with the customer.

2. Information Search:

Once a need is recognized, customers begin searching for information to address their problem. This can involve internal searches (recalling past experiences) or external searches (seeking information from friends, online reviews, etc.).

- **Sales Implication**: Sales professionals should provide easy access to relevant information about their products, including detailed descriptions, testimonials, and comparisons.

3. Evaluation of Alternatives:

After gathering information, customers evaluate different options based on various criteria, such as price, quality, features, and brand reputation.

- **Sales Implication**: Sales professionals should be prepared to highlight the unique selling points of their products and address any comparisons the customer may make with competitors.

4. Purchase Decision:

This is the stage where customers decide which product to purchase. Influencing factors at this stage include promotional offers, sales tactics, and the salesperson's ability to address any lingering objections.

- **Sales Implication**: Effective closing techniques and overcoming objections are critical at this stage. Sales professionals should be confident and persuasive.

5. Post-Purchase Behavior:

After the purchase, customers evaluate their decision based on their satisfaction with the product. This can lead to repeat purchases or negative word-of-mouth if they are dissatisfied.

- **Sales Implication**: Following up with customers post-purchase can help ensure satisfaction, address any issues, and foster loyalty.

8.4 Leveraging Customer Behavior Insights in Sales

To enhance sales effectiveness, professionals should leverage insights gained from understanding customer behavior:

1. Tailoring Sales Pitches:

By understanding the unique motivations and preferences of different customer segments, sales professionals can tailor their pitches to resonate more deeply.

- **Example**: For price-sensitive customers, emphasize discounts and value. For status-driven customers, focus on prestige and exclusivity.

2. Building Strong Relationships:

Understanding social influences and emotional triggers can help sales professionals build deeper connections with customers.

- **Example**: Use personalized communication and follow-ups to create a sense of community and loyalty.

3. Creating Compelling Content:

Sales and marketing teams can work together to create content that addresses customer pain points and motivations, enhancing the overall customer experience.

- **Example**: Develop educational resources or testimonials that highlight how your product solves common problems.

4. Utilizing Customer Feedback:

Gathering and analyzing customer feedback provides insights into their experiences, allowing for continuous improvement in products and services.

- **Example**: Conduct surveys or use social media to gather insights on customer satisfaction and areas for improvement.

Understanding customer behavior and the decision-making process is essential for sales professionals. By recognizing the psychological, social, and emotional factors that influence purchasing decisions, salespeople can tailor their approaches to meet customer needs effectively. Mastery of the decision-making stages enables sales professionals to engage customers more meaningfully and foster long-term relationships. Ultimately, leveraging insights into customer behavior can lead to improved sales performance, enhanced customer satisfaction, and increased loyalty, setting the foundation for sustained success in a competitive marketplace.

Chapter 9
Advanced Negotiation Skills in Sales

Negotiation is a core element of sales, yet it often extends beyond simply agreeing on price. A successful negotiator understands not just the technical aspects of negotiation but also the psychological dynamics that influence both parties. This chapter explores advanced negotiation techniques, backed by psychology, and helps you navigate complex sales situations, close deals effectively, and build long-lasting relationships with clients.

9.1 The Art of Negotiation in Sales

Negotiation in sales is not about winning or losing; it's about finding a mutually beneficial solution that satisfies both the salesperson and the customer. A strong negotiation skillset enables the salesperson to create value, adjust terms, and close deals in a way that leaves the customer feeling heard, understood, and appreciated.

- **Understanding Interests, Not Just Positions**: One of the first steps in any successful negotiation is understanding the difference between interests and positions. Positions are the specific terms or outcomes each party wants, while interests represent the underlying needs or desires driving those positions. For example, a customer may want a lower price (position), but their true interest may be getting more value for their budget. By focusing on interests, the salesperson can uncover creative solutions that satisfy both parties.

- **Collaborative vs. Competitive Approaches**: Sales negotiations can take either a collaborative or competitive approach. The collaborative approach focuses on cooperation and win-win solutions, while the competitive approach is more adversarial, where each side aims to claim as much value as possible. Successful negotiators lean towards a collaborative model, fostering long-term relationships and repeat business.

9.2 Psychological Principles Behind Effective Negotiation

Several psychological principles come into play during a negotiation, influencing how both parties perceive the value of the deal and each other. Understanding these principles is key to achieving better outcomes.

- **Anchoring**: Anchoring occurs when the first piece of information presented in a negotiation (often the first offer) influences subsequent discussions. By setting an initial offer that's reasonable but slightly higher than the target price, the salesperson can influence the customer's perception of what is fair and acceptable.

- **Reciprocity**: Humans have an innate tendency to return favors. This principle of reciprocity is a powerful tool in negotiation. Offering something small (like an added benefit or minor concession) early in the negotiation can encourage the customer to reciprocate with their own concessions, leading to a more favorable outcome for the salesperson.

- **Framing**: The way an offer is framed can significantly impact how it's perceived. For example, presenting a discount as "a special offer" or "limited-time deal" can create urgency and make the customer feel they are getting a better deal. Framing can also involve how risks are presented—whether they are seen as potential losses or opportunities.

- **Social Proof**: People tend to follow the actions of others, especially in situations where they are uncertain. Citing the success or satisfaction of other customers can help persuade the current customer that the offer is a good decision. This principle taps into the customer's fear of missing out (FOMO) and aligns with herd behavior.

9.3 Managing Buyer Resistance and Objections

It's normal for buyers to resist certain aspects of a sales proposal or raise objections during the negotiation. Handling these objections effectively can make or break the deal.

- **Active Listening and Empathy**: Listening actively and showing empathy are essential tools for understanding the root of the buyer's resistance. When a salesperson listens attentively and validates the buyer's concerns, it builds trust and creates an environment where the customer feels safe sharing their doubts.

- **Reframing Objections**: Rather than confronting objections directly, effective negotiators reframe them. For example, if a customer objects to the price, the salesperson might respond by discussing the long-term value and return on investment, shifting the focus from price to value.

- **The "Feel, Felt, Found" Technique**: This classic technique helps deal with objections by acknowledging the customer's concerns, sharing a similar experience, and offering a solution. For example: "I understand how you feel. Many of our clients have felt the same way. What they found, however, was that the value of the product far outweighed the initial investment."

9.4 The Power of Reciprocity and Concessions

Negotiations often involve giving up something in return for getting something else. The principle of reciprocity can be used to make concessions feel more impactful, while still securing your interests.

- **Strategic Concessions**: Concessions should never be made impulsively. They need to be strategic, and each one should be tied to a specific benefit for the salesperson. For example, a salesperson might offer a small discount in exchange for a commitment to a longer-term contract.

- **"Reciprocal Concessions"**: When making a concession, ask for something in return. For instance, after offering a slight price reduction, the salesperson might ask the customer to sign the deal immediately or agree to a slightly higher purchase volume. This balances the scales and ensures the salesperson doesn't lose value.

- **Giving to Get**: Sometimes, giving small, unexpected perks (such as a complimentary service or an additional product feature) can create a sense of goodwill and prompt the customer to reciprocate by accepting the deal. These gestures don't have to be large but should add value to the customer's overall experience.

9.5 How to Read Non-Verbal Cues in Negotiations

Non-verbal communication is a powerful tool in any negotiation. Understanding body language, tone of voice, and facial expressions can provide valuable insights into a buyer's thoughts, allowing the salesperson to adjust their approach accordingly.

- **Body Language**: Positive signs of interest include leaning forward, maintaining eye contact, and open posture. Negative signs, such as crossed arms or looking away, might indicate discomfort or resistance. By being attuned to these cues, a salesperson can adjust their approach—whether by softening their tone, changing tactics, or giving the buyer more space.

- **Tone of Voice**: A customer's tone can reveal their emotional state and level of engagement. A slow or hesitant tone may signal doubt or uncertainty, while an enthusiastic tone might indicate excitement or readiness to move forward.

- **Facial Expressions**: Subtle facial expressions can often convey more than words. A raised eyebrow, slight smile, or frown can tell you whether the customer is feeling positive or negative about the offer. Being observant of these can help a salesperson steer the negotiation in the right direction.

9.6 High-Pressure Sales Situations: Staying Calm and Strategic

Salespeople often face high-pressure situations, whether it's a looming deadline, competing offers, or a customer pushing for last-minute concessions. Staying calm and strategic is key.

- **Maintaining Emotional Control**: High-pressure situations can trigger emotional reactions, but experienced negotiators know how to remain composed. This doesn't mean suppressing feelings but rather recognizing emotional triggers and using them to stay focused and make rational decisions.
- **Time as a Tool**: Time can be an asset in high-pressure negotiations. If a customer is rushing, the salesperson can use time to their advantage by remaining patient, allowing the customer to feel heard, and using the extra time to strengthen their argument or offer additional value.
- **Anchoring Under Pressure**: In high-pressure situations, anchoring is even more powerful. By setting the right expectations early in the negotiation, salespeople can prevent the customer from making unreasonable demands as time progresses.

9.7 Closing Deals: When and How to Seal the Agreement

The final stage of any negotiation is the close. Knowing when and how to close the deal is critical for successful outcomes.

- **Recognizing Buying Signals**: Buyers often give subtle cues that they're ready to close the deal, such as asking for final details, showing eagerness to finalize the terms, or discussing logistics. Recognizing these signals can help the salesperson transition smoothly into closing the deal.

- **Trial Close**: A trial close is a question that helps gauge the buyer's readiness to make a decision. Examples include: "How does this sound so far?" or "Are you ready to move forward with this?" These questions can reveal any lingering concerns and allow the salesperson to address them before officially closing.

- **Assumptive Close**: The assumptive close involves assuming the deal is done and moving forward as if the buyer has already made the decision. This could be something like: "Great! Let's get the paperwork started so we can deliver by next week."

- **Urgency Close**: Creating a sense of urgency can spur the customer to act quickly. This may involve offering a limited-time discount or emphasizing the benefits of making the purchase now rather than later.

Mastering negotiation in sales requires a deep understanding of psychological principles, strategic thinking, and emotional intelligence. By leveraging these advanced techniques, salespeople can manage buyer resistance, make strategic concessions, and close deals in a way that benefits both parties. With practice, these skills will not only help you negotiate better deals but also build stronger, more trusting relationships with your clients.

Chapter 10
The Psychology of Consumer Decision-Making

Introduction

Consumer decision-making is a complex process influenced by a variety of psychological, emotional, and cognitive factors. Understanding the psychology behind how and why people make purchasing decisions is crucial for sales professionals aiming to influence their customers effectively. This chapter explores the stages of the decision-making process, the psychological biases at play, and strategies to guide consumers toward favorable decisions.

10.1 Understanding the Consumer Decision-Making Process

Consumers typically go through a series of steps when making a purchasing decision. The process can be broken down into five stages:

1. **Need Recognition**: The decision-making process starts when a consumer recognizes a problem or need. This could be triggered by internal stimuli (e.g., hunger, thirst) or external stimuli (e.g., advertising, a recommendation from a friend). Sales professionals must identify the needs their product or service can fulfill and position their offering as the solution.

2. **Information Search**: Once the need is recognized, the consumer searches for information to find potential solutions. This could involve looking online, asking for recommendations, or visiting stores. Consumers often rely on trusted sources, such as reviews, recommendations, or expert opinions.

3. **Evaluation of Alternatives**: Consumers then compare different options based on factors such as price, features, quality, and brand reputation. The evaluation stage is where consumers weigh the pros and cons of each alternative.

4. **Purchase Decision**: After evaluating alternatives, the consumer makes a decision. However, external factors like sales pressure, promotions, or brand loyalty can influence this decision.

5. **Post-Purchase Behavior**: Following the purchase, the consumer assesses their satisfaction with the product or service. If satisfied, they are likely to become repeat customers and may recommend the product to others. If dissatisfied, they may seek a return or complain.

Understanding this process is vital for tailoring sales strategies at each stage, ensuring the consumer's needs are addressed and guiding them toward a positive decision.

10.2 The Role of Cognitive Biases in Consumer Choices

Consumers are not always entirely rational when making purchasing decisions. Various cognitive biases influence their choices:

1. **Anchoring Bias**: Consumers tend to rely heavily on the first piece of information they receive when making a

decision, such as the initial price offered or the first product they see. Salespeople can use this by presenting higher-priced items first, making the subsequent options seem like a better deal.

2. **Confirmation Bias**: Consumers seek information that confirms their preexisting beliefs and values. Sales professionals can use this bias by emphasizing aspects of their product that align with the customer's values or needs, even if the product offers a wider range of features.

3. **Social Proof**: People tend to follow the actions of others. When a product or service is recommended by friends, family, or even online reviews, consumers are more likely to trust and choose it. Incorporating testimonials and reviews into marketing and sales efforts can tap into this powerful bias.

4. **Loss Aversion**: The pain of losing something is psychologically more powerful than the pleasure of gaining something of equal value. This bias can be leveraged in sales by framing offers in terms of what the consumer stands to lose if they don't act now (e.g., limited-time discounts, limited stock).

5. **Scarcity Effect**: Consumers perceive scarce items as more valuable. Limited-time offers, "only a few left" messages, or exclusivity can create urgency and encourage faster decision-making.

10.3 How Emotions Influence Purchases

Emotions play a huge role in consumer decisions. While logic and reasoning are involved, emotions often drive final decisions. Sales professionals can harness the emotional triggers that influence purchasing behavior:

1. **Fear of Missing Out (FOMO)**: Consumers often make purchases due to a fear of missing out on a great deal or experience. Sales strategies that include urgency and exclusivity tap into this emotion, prompting consumers to act before the opportunity is gone.

2. **Trust and Security**: Consumers feel more comfortable making a purchase when they trust the brand. Trust can be built through transparency, customer service, and delivering on promises. A sense of security also comes from clear return policies and guarantees.

3. **Happiness and Aspiration**: Positive emotions like happiness, excitement, and the feeling of success often influence buying decisions. Consumers buy products that they believe will bring them joy, elevate their status, or help them achieve personal goals. Marketing messages that highlight how a product enhances the customer's lifestyle or fulfills their aspirations can resonate deeply.

4. **Nostalgia**: The feeling of nostalgia can trigger consumer decisions when products evoke past memories or emotional connections. Brands can use nostalgia by emphasizing timeless quality, heritage, or using nostalgic imagery in their marketing.

10.4 The Impact of Social Proof on Buying Behavior

Social proof is the psychological phenomenon where people look to others' actions to guide their own behavior. In sales, social proof can take many forms:

1. **Testimonials and Reviews**: Customers are more likely to purchase a product when they see that others have had a positive experience with it. Incorporating testimonials, case studies, and user-generated content into the sales process provides powerful social proof.
2. **Influencers and Celebrity Endorsements**: Many consumers look to influencers or celebrities for buying guidance. Endorsements from trusted figures can lend credibility to a product and encourage consumers to make a purchase.
3. **User Counts and Popularity Metrics**: Displaying the number of users or customers who have purchased a product or service reinforces its value. For example, showing that "10,000 people have already bought this product" can persuade others to follow suit.

10.5 Building a Persuasive Argument for Buyers

The key to influencing consumer decision-making is crafting a persuasive argument that resonates with the consumer's needs, emotions, and decision-making process. Here's how to build that argument:

1. **Focus on Benefits, Not Features**: Consumers care about how a product will solve their problem or improve their lives. Emphasizing the benefits of your product—rather than just its features—will make it more appealing.
2. **Use Stories and Testimonials**: Personal stories and testimonials help build a connection between the consumer and the product. Storytelling engages emotions and can make the product seem more relatable and desirable.

3. **Overcome Objections**: Address common objections directly during the sales process. Understand the concerns that customers may have and present solutions. This can reduce hesitation and increase the likelihood of a sale.

4. **Create a Sense of Urgency**: Use psychological triggers like scarcity, time-limited offers, or exclusive deals to create a sense of urgency, prompting quicker decision-making.

10.6 Decision Fatigue: How to Simplify Choices

Decision fatigue occurs when consumers are overwhelmed by too many options. This can result in procrastination or poor decision-making. Sales professionals can combat this by:

1. **Limiting Options**: Offering fewer choices reduces cognitive overload. For example, instead of presenting ten different models of a product, narrow it down to the top three most relevant options for the consumer.

2. **Streamlining the Decision Process**: Make the decision-making process easier by highlighting the most important aspects of the product and guiding the consumer through the benefits.

3. **Providing Clear Recommendations**: Offering clear recommendations and "best-choice" options helps consumers make faster decisions by providing guidance and reducing the amount of cognitive work they need to do.

10.7 The Post-Purchase Decision: Building Customer Loyalty

The purchasing process doesn't end with the sale. Post-purchase behavior plays a crucial role in retaining customers and fostering brand loyalty. Sales professionals can encourage repeat business by:

1. **Follow-Up Communication**: Sending follow-up emails or surveys to check on customer satisfaction shows that the business cares about the consumer's experience.

2. **Offer Additional Value**: Offering complementary products, loyalty programs, or discounts on future purchases can encourage customers to return and make additional purchases.

3. **Ask for Reviews and Referrals**: Satisfied customers are more likely to leave positive reviews or refer friends. Encourage this behavior by asking for feedback or offering incentives for referrals.

Understanding consumer decision-making from a psychological perspective is essential for sales professionals. By recognizing the cognitive biases, emotional triggers, and decision-making processes that drive purchasing behavior, salespeople can tailor their approach to meet consumer needs and influence their choices more effectively. Whether you're guiding a customer through the initial stages of need recognition or handling post-purchase loyalty, a deep understanding of consumer psychology is a powerful tool in boosting sales success.

Chapter 11
Cross-Cultural Sales Psychology

11.1 Understanding Cultural Differences in Sales Psychology

Cultural differences play a significant role in how individuals perceive sales messages, how they make decisions, and how they react to various sales tactics. Understanding these differences is crucial for tailoring sales strategies to specific markets.

Key Points:

- **Cultural Context**: High-context cultures (such as Japan, China, and many Arab countries) rely heavily on implicit communication and context, while low-context cultures (like the United States, Germany, and Scandinavia) value explicit and direct communication.

- **Individualism vs. Collectivism**: Cultures that emphasize individualism (such as the U.S. and much of Western Europe) focus on personal success, independence, and individual goals. In contrast, collectivist cultures (such as many Asian and Latin American countries) place more value on group harmony, community, and interdependence.

- **Power Distance**: In high power-distance cultures (like India, Mexico, and much of the Middle East), hierarchies and authority are respected, and salespeople may need to approach senior decision-makers directly. In low power-distance cultures (such as Denmark or New Zealand), decision-making is more egalitarian, and building relationships at all levels of an organization is crucial.

- **Communication Styles**: Direct versus indirect communication styles can significantly impact how a message is received. In cultures with an indirect communication style, like Japan or some Middle Eastern countries, subtlety, politeness, and non-verbal cues are essential to avoid offense.

11.2 Cultural Norms and Their Impact on Buying Behavior

Cultural norms shape buying behavior in profound ways. Understanding these cultural patterns can help salespeople anticipate how potential customers will react to certain types of messaging and offers.

Key Points:

- **Status and Luxury Goods**: In some cultures, like China and parts of the Middle East, luxury goods are often purchased as symbols of status. This means that marketing strategies may need to emphasize exclusivity, prestige, and success.
- **Price Sensitivity**: Cultures with a high degree of price sensitivity, such as many European or South American countries, may focus more on value and affordability in their purchasing decisions. These cultures may favor discounts, promotions, and bundles.

- **Group Decision-Making**: In collectivist cultures, purchasing decisions are often made by a group or family. Sales strategies in these cultures may need to emphasize how a product benefits the collective, focusing on group needs over individual desires.
- **The Role of Rituals**: Some cultures, like those in India and parts of Southeast Asia, have strong ties to ritual and tradition. Products that align with or respect these rituals—such as food items or religious goods—may have an emotional appeal that others do not.

11.3 Adapting Sales Approaches for Different Markets

Adapting a sales approach to different cultures involves understanding the unique expectations and preferences of each market. Successful global sales strategies involve a high degree of flexibility and customization.

Key Points:

- **Localizing Marketing Content**: Sales materials should be localized not just by language but also by considering cultural symbols, colors, and imagery. For instance, while white may symbolize purity in Western cultures, it's associated with mourning in some Asian cultures.
- **Personalization**: In collectivist cultures, building personal relationships before discussing business is vital. In individualist cultures, customers may appreciate a more straightforward, business-first approach.
- **Product Customization**: Ensure that products are culturally appropriate. For example, food products may

need to adjust their ingredients or packaging to suit local tastes or dietary restrictions (e.g., halal, kosher, or vegetarian preferences).
- **Sales Tactics**: In some cultures, aggressive sales tactics may be seen as pushy or inappropriate. For example, aggressive upselling is less acceptable in Japan or Sweden, whereas it may work in the U.S. or Latin America.

11.4 Cross-Cultural Communication in Sales

Effective communication in cross-cultural settings involves understanding not just language but also non-verbal cues, body language, and tone of voice. Misunderstandings can arise from seemingly minor cultural differences.

Key Points:
- **Non-Verbal Communication**: Body language, gestures, eye contact, and even personal space vary significantly across cultures. For example, in the U.S., maintaining eye contact is often a sign of confidence, while in some Asian cultures, it may be seen as a sign of disrespect.
- **Tone and Formality**: The level of formality used in communication varies. For example, in countries like Germany or Japan, formal language and titles are expected in business communication. In contrast, American and Australian business cultures tend to be more informal.
- **Language Barriers**: Even within countries where the same language is spoken, regional dialects and colloquialisms can create confusion. When working

internationally, it's crucial to simplify language and avoid idiomatic expressions that might not translate well.

11.5 Building Trust Across Cultures

Trust is a fundamental part of any business transaction, but it's developed differently depending on the cultural context. Understanding how trust is built in various cultures will help you navigate relationships more effectively.

Key Points:

- **Slow vs. Fast Trust Building**: In high-context cultures, building trust can take time, and it is often based on personal relationships. In low-context cultures, trust may be built more quickly, often through logical, evidence-based communication.

- **Reliability and Reputation**: In cultures like Japan and Germany, reputation and reliability are paramount. Salespeople need to establish credibility by providing evidence of the product's quality, and often, referrals from trusted sources are essential.

- **Long-Term Relationships**: In collectivist cultures, it is important to demonstrate commitment to long-term relationships. In contrast, Western sales approaches may place more focus on transactional interactions and immediate outcomes.

11.6 Tailoring Emotional Appeals for International Audiences

Emotions influence decisions differently in various cultures. While some emotions, like happiness or fear, may be universally understood, others may resonate more strongly in specific cultural contexts.

Key Points:

- **Emotional Appeal to Family Values**: In cultures where family is central (e.g., India, Latin America), marketing messages that appeal to family values, security, and well-being tend to be more effective.

- **Fear of Loss**: In some cultures, like the U.S. and other Western countries, fear-based marketing (e.g., missing out on an opportunity or benefit) is highly effective. In other cultures, such as Japan, subtlety and respect for individual choice may be more effective.

- **Respect and Honor**: In cultures such as those in the Middle East or East Asia, appeals to honor, respect, and social status are potent motivators in decision-making.

11.7 Global vs. Local: Striking the Right Balance in Sales Strategies

One of the challenges in cross-cultural sales is determining how much to standardize and how much to localize. Global strategies can save costs and streamline operations, but they may not always be effective in local markets.

Key Points:

- **Global Brand Identity vs. Local Adaptation**: A strong global brand identity is crucial for consistency across markets, but local adaptations are often necessary to meet cultural needs. Companies like McDonald's and Coca-Cola have successfully adapted their products while maintaining their global brand image.

- **Cost vs. Customization**: Customizing products, marketing materials, and sales approaches for each local market can be costly, but the return on investment may be significant. Global brands must weigh the trade-off between standardization and customization.

11.8 Case Studies of Successful Cross-Cultural Sales Campaigns

Looking at real-world examples helps bring theory to life. Here are a few companies that have successfully navigated cross-cultural sales challenges:

- **McDonald's**: McDonald's adapts its menu in different countries to meet local tastes and cultural preferences, such as offering the "McAloo Tikki" in India or "Teriyaki Burgers" in Japan. This approach allows the brand to remain globally recognizable while appealing to local preferences.
- **Coca-Cola**: Coca-Cola has had significant success in adapting its marketing to local cultures. In India, for example, Coca-Cola's marketing focuses on the idea of bringing people together in joyous, festive settings, which resonates with the cultural value of community.
- **Apple**: Apple is another brand that balances global consistency with local adaptation. It maintains a premium brand image across cultures but adjusts its marketing messages to appeal to local values—like family and status in China, or environmental consciousness in Sweden.

Cross-cultural sales psychology is a critical component of global business success. By understanding the cultural differences in consumer behavior, communication styles, trust-building, and emotional appeals, sales professionals can tailor their strategies to effectively engage with diverse international audiences. The ability to adapt to cultural nuances is not only an advantage but often a necessity in today's interconnected world.

Chapter 12

Leveraging Technology and Data in Sales

In the rapidly evolving landscape of sales, technology and data have become essential tools for sales professionals. This chapter will explore how technology and data analytics can enhance sales strategies, improve customer interactions, and drive overall sales performance. By leveraging the right tools and insights, sales professionals can make informed decisions, personalize their approaches, and ultimately achieve better results.

12.1 The Role of Technology in Sales

1. Customer Relationship Management (CRM) Systems

CRM systems are software platforms that help sales professionals manage customer interactions, track leads, and organize data. These systems centralize customer information, making it easier to understand customer needs and preferences.

- **Benefits of CRM**:
    - Streamlined communication with customers.
    - Enhanced tracking of sales activities and performance metrics.
    - Improved collaboration among sales teams.

2. Sales Automation Tools

Sales automation tools help streamline repetitive tasks, allowing sales professionals to focus on building relationships and closing deals. These tools can automate lead scoring, email campaigns, follow-ups, and more.

- **Benefits of Sales Automation**:
    - Increased efficiency by reducing time spent on administrative tasks.
    - Consistency in customer communication and follow-ups.
    - Enhanced lead management and nurturing processes.

3. Communication and Collaboration Tools

Modern communication tools, such as video conferencing platforms, instant messaging apps, and collaboration software, enable seamless communication among sales teams and with customers.

- **Benefits of Communication Tools**:
    - Improved real-time collaboration and information sharing.
    - Enhanced customer engagement through virtual meetings and demos.
    - Greater flexibility in communication, accommodating diverse preferences.

12.2 Utilizing Data Analytics in Sales

Data analytics involves examining data to extract meaningful insights that can inform decision-making. In sales, data analytics can provide valuable information about customer behavior, preferences, and market trends.

1. Understanding Customer Behavior

Analyzing customer data helps sales professionals understand buying patterns, preferences, and pain points. This information can guide sales strategies and improve targeting efforts.

- **Benefits of Customer Behavior Analysis**:
    - Identification of high-value customers and segments.
    - Insights into the effectiveness of sales tactics and messaging.
    - Opportunities for personalized marketing and sales approaches.

2. Sales Performance Metrics

Tracking sales performance metrics allows sales professionals to evaluate their effectiveness and identify areas for improvement. Key performance indicators (KPIs) may include conversion rates, average deal size, and sales cycle length.

- **Benefits of Performance Metrics**:
    - Data-driven insights into individual and team performance.
    - Ability to set realistic sales goals and benchmarks.
    - Identification of trends that inform future sales strategies.

3. Predictive Analytics

Predictive analytics uses historical data and statistical algorithms to forecast future outcomes. In sales, this can help identify potential leads, predict customer behavior, and optimize sales strategies.

- **Benefits of Predictive Analytics**:
    - Improved lead scoring and prioritization.
    - Anticipation of customer needs and preferences.
    - Enhanced targeting of marketing efforts based on predicted trends.

12.3 Personalizing Sales Interactions with Technology

Personalization is crucial for creating meaningful customer interactions. Technology enables sales professionals to tailor their approaches based on individual customer preferences and behaviors.

1. Targeted Marketing Campaigns

Using data analytics, sales teams can create targeted marketing campaigns that resonate with specific customer segments. Personalizing messages based on customer demographics, interests, and previous interactions increases engagement.

- **Benefits of Targeted Campaigns**:
    - Higher response rates and engagement levels.
    - Improved customer experience through relevant offers.

- Enhanced brand loyalty by addressing specific needs.

2. Customized Sales Presentations

Sales professionals can leverage technology to create customized presentations and proposals tailored to each customer's unique needs and pain points.

- **Benefits of Customized Presentations**:
    - Greater relevance and impact during sales meetings.
    - Increased likelihood of addressing customer objections.
    - Enhanced customer perception of the salesperson's dedication and expertise.

3. Follow-Up Automation

Automating follow-up communications allows sales professionals to maintain consistent contact with customers. Personalized follow-up emails or messages can be tailored based on the customer's previous interactions and preferences.

- **Benefits of Follow-Up Automation**:
    - Timely and relevant follow-ups enhance customer engagement.
    - Reduced risk of losing leads due to lack of communication.
    - Opportunity to provide additional value through relevant content.

12.4 Embracing Emerging Technologies

Emerging technologies continue to shape the future of sales. Sales professionals must stay informed about these trends and be willing to adapt to new tools and methodologies.

1. Artificial Intelligence (AI) in Sales

AI technologies can enhance various aspects of the sales process, from lead generation to customer support. AI can analyze vast amounts of data, provide insights, and automate routine tasks.

- **Benefits of AI in Sales**:
    - Enhanced lead scoring and prioritization based on data analysis.
    - Automation of customer interactions through chatbots and virtual assistants.
    - Predictive insights that inform sales strategies and decision-making.

2. Virtual Reality (VR) and Augmented Reality (AR)

VR and AR technologies can enhance customer experiences by providing immersive product demonstrations and virtual tours. These technologies allow customers to visualize products in a realistic setting.

- **Benefits of VR and AR in Sales**:
    - Improved customer engagement and understanding of products.
    - Unique selling experiences that differentiate the brand.

- Increased confidence in purchasing decisions through realistic visualization.

3. Social Selling

Social selling leverages social media platforms to connect with potential customers and build relationships. Sales professionals can use social media to share valuable content, engage with customers, and identify leads.

- **Benefits of Social Selling**:
    - Expanded reach and visibility to potential customers.
    - Opportunities for authentic engagement and relationship building.
    - Access to valuable customer insights based on social interactions.

12.5 Implementing Technology and Data in Your Sales Strategy

1. Identify Your Goals

Begin by defining your sales goals and objectives. Understanding what you want to achieve will help you determine which technologies and data analytics tools will best support your strategy.

2. Choose the Right Tools

Research and select the tools and technologies that align with your sales objectives. Consider factors such as ease of use, integration capabilities, and scalability.

- **Examples of Useful Tools**:
    - CRM platforms (e.g., Salesforce, HubSpot)

- Sales automation tools (e.g., Outreach, Yesware)
- Data analytics tools (e.g., Tableau, Google Analytics)

3. Train Your Team

Invest in training for your sales team to ensure they understand how to use the chosen tools effectively. Ongoing training and support can enhance adoption and maximize the benefits of technology.

4. Analyze and Optimize

Regularly analyze the data generated from your sales efforts and adjust your strategies as needed. Use insights from performance metrics to inform decision-making and drive continuous improvement.

Leveraging technology and data in sales is no longer optional; it is essential for success in today's competitive landscape. By embracing tools such as CRM systems, sales automation, and data analytics, sales professionals can enhance their effectiveness, personalize customer interactions, and make informed decisions. As technology continues to evolve, staying abreast of emerging trends will empower sales teams to adapt and thrive. Ultimately, integrating technology and data into the sales process will lead to improved customer experiences, increased sales performance, and sustainable business growth. By harnessing the power of technology and data, sales professionals can elevate their strategies and drive success in an ever-changing marketplace.

Chapter 13

Building and Managing a High-Performance Sales Team

Creating a high-performance sales team is essential for achieving organizational goals and driving revenue growth. This chapter will explore the key elements of building and managing an effective sales team, including recruitment strategies, training and development, performance management, and fostering a positive sales culture.

13.1 Understanding the High-Performance Sales Team

1. Defining a High-Performance Sales Team

A high-performance sales team consistently meets or exceeds sales targets, demonstrates a strong understanding of the market and customer needs, and collaborates effectively to drive results. Such teams are characterized by:

- Clear roles and responsibilities.
- Strong communication and collaboration.
- A commitment to continuous improvement.
- High levels of motivation and engagement.

2. The Importance of a High-Performance Sales Team

High-performance sales teams can significantly impact an organization's success. They drive revenue growth, improve customer satisfaction, and enhance brand reputation. Building a strong sales team is crucial for maintaining a competitive edge in the marketplace.

13.2 Recruitment Strategies for Building a High-Performance Sales Team

1. Identifying the Right Traits and Skills

When recruiting for a sales team, it is essential to identify the traits and skills that align with the organization's goals. Look for candidates who exhibit:

- Strong communication and interpersonal skills.
- Resilience and adaptability.
- A track record of meeting or exceeding sales targets.
- A customer-focused mindset.

2. Crafting an Attractive Job Description

Create a clear and compelling job description that outlines the responsibilities, qualifications, and expectations for the role. Highlight the organization's culture, values, and opportunities for growth to attract top talent.

3. Utilizing Diverse Recruitment Channels

Use a variety of recruitment channels to reach a broader audience. Consider leveraging:

- Job boards and recruitment websites.
- Social media platforms (LinkedIn, Twitter, etc.).
- Employee referrals and networking events.
- Recruitment agencies specializing in sales roles.

4. Conducting Effective Interviews

Develop a structured interview process that assesses candidates' skills, experiences, and cultural fit. Consider incorporating:

- Behavioral interview questions to gauge past performance.
- Role-playing exercises to evaluate sales skills.
- Assessments or tests to measure sales acumen and problem-solving abilities.

13.3 Training and Development for Sales Excellence

1. Onboarding and Orientation

A comprehensive onboarding process is essential for helping new sales team members acclimate to the organization and understand its products, services, and sales processes. Ensure that the onboarding program includes:

- Company culture and values.
- Product training and sales methodologies.
- An overview of tools and resources available to the sales team.

2. Ongoing Training and Skill Development

Continuous training and development are vital for maintaining high performance. Offer regular training sessions on:

- Product knowledge and updates.
- Sales techniques and best practices.
- Market trends and customer insights.

Utilize various training formats, such as workshops, webinars, and e-learning platforms, to accommodate different learning styles.

3. Coaching and Mentoring

Establish a coaching and mentoring program to support sales team members in their professional development. Encourage experienced team members to mentor newer employees, sharing insights and strategies for success.

- **Benefits of Coaching and Mentoring**:
    - Personalized support and guidance.
    - Increased confidence and motivation.
    - Knowledge sharing and best practice dissemination.

13.4 Performance Management in Sales Teams

1. Setting Clear Goals and Expectations

Establish clear performance goals and expectations for each sales team member. Ensure that these goals align with the overall objectives of the organization and are specific, measurable, achievable, relevant, and time-bound (SMART).

2. Regular Performance Reviews

Conduct regular performance reviews to assess individual and team performance. Provide constructive feedback, recognize achievements, and identify areas for improvement.

- **Key Performance Indicators (KPIs) to Monitor**:
    - Sales revenue and growth.
    - Conversion rates and lead generation.

o Customer retention and satisfaction metrics.

3. Rewarding High Performance

Recognize and reward high-performing sales team members to reinforce desired behaviors and motivate the team. Consider implementing:

- Incentive programs, such as bonuses or commissions.
- Recognition programs that highlight achievements (e.g., "Salesperson of the Month").
- Career advancement opportunities for top performers.

13.5 Fostering a Positive Sales Culture

1. Creating an Inclusive Environment

Foster an inclusive and supportive sales culture that values diversity and encourages collaboration. Promote open communication, teamwork, and respect among team members.

2. Encouraging Collaboration

Encourage collaboration within the sales team and across departments. Establish regular team meetings to share insights, discuss challenges, and celebrate successes.

- **Benefits of Collaboration**:
    - o Enhanced problem-solving and innovation.
    - o Improved knowledge sharing and resource utilization.
    - o Strengthened relationships among team members.

3. Promoting Work-Life Balance

Recognize the importance of work-life balance in maintaining employee well-being and satisfaction. Encourage flexible working arrangements and promote self-care practices.

- **Strategies for Promoting Work-Life Balance**:
    - Offer flexible scheduling options.
    - Provide resources for stress management and wellness.
    - Encourage regular breaks and time off.

13.6 Adapting to Change and Challenges

1. Embracing Change

Sales teams must be adaptable to thrive in a constantly evolving business environment. Encourage a growth mindset that embraces change and innovation.

- **Strategies for Embracing Change**:
    - Communicate the benefits of change and new initiatives.
    - Involve team members in the decision-making process.
    - Provide training and support for adapting to new technologies or processes.

2. Addressing Challenges and Obstacles

Identify and address challenges that may hinder team performance. Regularly solicit feedback from team members to understand their concerns and provide solutions.

- **Common Challenges to Address**:
    - High turnover rates.
    - Inadequate training and resources.
    - Lack of motivation or engagement.

Building and managing a high-performance sales team requires a strategic approach that encompasses effective recruitment, ongoing training and development, performance management, and fostering a positive sales culture. By focusing on these key elements, sales leaders can create a motivated, skilled, and engaged team capable of achieving exceptional results. As the sales landscape continues to evolve, adapting to changes and challenges will ensure that the sales team remains agile and competitive. Ultimately, investing in the development and well-being of the sales team will lead to improved performance, greater customer satisfaction, and long-term success for the organization. By prioritizing the creation of a high-performance sales team, organizations can position themselves for growth and success in an ever-changing marketplace.

Chapter 14
Sales Strategy Development and Implementation

Developing a robust sales strategy is vital for achieving long-term success and meeting organizational objectives. This chapter explores the key components of effective sales strategy development and implementation, including market analysis, target audience identification, value proposition creation, and tactical execution.

14.1 Understanding Sales Strategy

1. Definition of Sales Strategy

A sales strategy is a comprehensive plan that outlines how an organization will sell its products or services to achieve its business goals. It encompasses various elements, including market positioning, target audiences, pricing strategies, and sales tactics. A well-defined sales strategy aligns with the overall business strategy and provides a roadmap for sales teams to follow.

2. The Importance of a Sales Strategy

An effective sales strategy serves several essential purposes:

- **Guides Sales Efforts**: Provides direction and clarity for sales teams, ensuring that their activities align with organizational goals.

- **Enhances Focus**: Helps prioritize efforts on high-value opportunities, optimizing resource allocation.
- **Facilitates Measurement**: Establishes benchmarks for success and enables tracking of performance metrics.
- **Drives Consistency**: Ensures a unified approach to selling across the organization.

14.2 Conducting Market Analysis

1. Analyzing Market Trends

Understanding market trends is crucial for developing a relevant sales strategy. Analyze the following aspects:

- **Industry Trends**: Identify changes in the industry landscape, such as emerging technologies, regulatory shifts, or economic factors affecting customer behavior.
- **Competitive Landscape**: Evaluate competitors' strengths, weaknesses, and market positioning. Analyze their products, pricing, and sales tactics to identify opportunities for differentiation.
- **Customer Preferences**: Research changing customer preferences and behaviors through surveys, interviews, and market research.

2. Identifying Opportunities and Threats

Utilize SWOT analysis (Strengths, Weaknesses, Opportunities, Threats) to evaluate the organization's position in the market. This analysis will help identify areas for growth and potential challenges.

- **Opportunities**: Look for gaps in the market, unmet customer needs, or emerging trends that the organization can capitalize on.

- **Threats**: Identify external factors that may pose challenges, such as increased competition, economic downturns, or changes in consumer behavior.

14.3 Identifying Target Audiences

1. Segmentation of Target Markets

Segmenting the target market involves dividing it into distinct groups based on shared characteristics, behaviors, or needs. Common segmentation criteria include:

- **Demographics**: Age, gender, income level, education, etc.
- **Geographics**: Location, climate, population density, etc.
- **Psychographics**: Lifestyle, values, interests, etc.
- **Behavioral Factors**: Purchasing behavior, brand loyalty, product usage, etc.

2. Developing Buyer Personas

Creating detailed buyer personas helps sales teams understand their ideal customers better. A buyer persona is a semi-fictional representation of a target customer based on data and insights. Each persona should include:

- **Demographic Information**: Age, gender, occupation, income level, etc.
- **Goals and Challenges**: What the customer aims to achieve and the obstacles they face.
- **Buying Preferences**: Preferred channels for purchasing and decision-making processes.

14.4 Crafting a Compelling Value Proposition

1. Defining the Value Proposition

A strong value proposition articulates the unique benefits and value that a product or service offers to customers. It should answer the following questions:

- **What problems does the product or service solve?**
- **What differentiates it from competitors?**
- **What benefits do customers gain by choosing this offering?**

2. Communicating the Value Proposition

The value proposition should be clearly communicated in all sales and marketing materials. Sales teams should be trained to effectively articulate the value proposition during customer interactions.

- **Tips for Effective Communication**:
    - Use clear and concise language.
    - Focus on customer benefits rather than product features.
    - Tailor the message to resonate with specific buyer personas.

14.5 Developing Sales Tactics and Execution Plans

1. Selecting Sales Tactics

Based on the defined sales strategy, choose the appropriate tactics to reach and engage target audiences. Common sales tactics include:

- **Direct Selling**: Personal interactions with potential customers through face-to-face meetings, phone calls, or virtual presentations.
- **Consultative Selling**: Focusing on understanding customer needs and providing tailored solutions.
- **Inbound Marketing**: Attracting leads through content marketing, social media, and SEO strategies.
- **Account-Based Selling**: Targeting specific high-value accounts with personalized outreach and solutions.

2. Creating an Implementation Plan

An effective implementation plan outlines the steps required to execute the sales strategy successfully. Key components include:

- **Timeline**: Establish a clear timeline for each phase of the strategy.
- **Resource Allocation**: Determine the resources needed, including personnel, budget, and tools.
- **Responsibilities**: Assign specific roles and responsibilities to team members to ensure accountability.

14.6 Monitoring and Measuring Performance

1. Defining Key Performance Indicators (KPIs)

Identify relevant KPIs to measure the effectiveness of the sales strategy. Common sales KPIs include:

- **Sales Revenue**: Total revenue generated over a specific period.

- **Conversion Rate**: Percentage of leads converted into customers.
- **Sales Cycle Length**: The average time it takes to close a sale.
- **Customer Acquisition Cost (CAC)**: The total cost of acquiring a new customer.

2. Conducting Regular Performance Reviews

Regularly review sales performance against established KPIs. Analyze results to determine what is working and where improvements are needed.

- **Adjusting the Strategy**: Based on performance data, be prepared to pivot and adjust the sales strategy as necessary. This may involve refining target audiences, revising messaging, or adopting new sales tactics.

14.7 Adapting to Market Changes

1. Staying Agile and Responsive

The sales landscape is constantly evolving. Sales teams must remain agile and responsive to changes in market conditions, customer preferences, and competitive dynamics.

- **Continuous Learning**: Encourage ongoing education and training for sales teams to stay updated on industry trends and best practices.

2. Gathering Feedback

Regularly solicit feedback from customers and sales team members to identify areas for improvement and inform future strategy adjustments.

- **Customer Feedback**: Conduct surveys or interviews to understand customer satisfaction and areas for enhancement.

- **Internal Feedback**: Encourage open communication within the sales team to gather insights on challenges faced during the sales process.

Developing and implementing an effective sales strategy is a critical component of achieving organizational success. By conducting thorough market analysis, identifying target audiences, crafting a compelling value proposition, and selecting appropriate sales tactics, organizations can create a roadmap for driving sales performance. Regularly monitoring and adjusting the strategy ensures that sales teams remain agile and responsive to market changes. Ultimately, a well-defined sales strategy empowers organizations to build strong customer relationships, increase revenue, and sustain a competitive advantage in an ever-changing marketplace. By investing in the development of a robust sales strategy, organizations can position themselves for long-term success and growth.

Chapter 15
Leveraging Technology in Sales

In today's fast-paced business environment, leveraging technology is crucial for sales success. This chapter explores the various technologies that can enhance sales processes, improve customer engagement, and drive overall performance. We will delve into the different types of sales technologies, their benefits, best practices for implementation, and future trends.

15.1 Understanding Sales Technology

1. Definition of Sales Technology

Sales technology refers to tools and software that assist sales teams in managing their activities, optimizing performance, and enhancing customer interactions. These technologies can streamline processes, improve communication, and provide valuable insights into customer behavior.

2. The Importance of Sales Technology

The right sales technology can significantly impact productivity, efficiency, and revenue growth. Key benefits include:

- **Increased Efficiency**: Automating repetitive tasks allows sales professionals to focus on high-value activities.

- **Enhanced Customer Insights**: Access to data analytics helps sales teams understand customer behavior and preferences.

- **Improved Collaboration**: Technology facilitates better communication and collaboration within sales teams and across departments.

- **Better Tracking and Reporting**: Sales technologies provide tools for tracking performance and generating reports to assess effectiveness.

15.2 Types of Sales Technologies

1. Customer Relationship Management (CRM) Systems

CRM systems are essential tools for managing customer relationships and interactions. They help sales teams track leads, manage contacts, and monitor sales pipelines. Key features of CRM systems include:

- **Lead Management**: Organizing and tracking leads throughout the sales process.

- **Contact Management**: Storing customer information and interaction history.

- **Sales Forecasting**: Predicting future sales based on historical data and trends.

Popular CRM Systems: Salesforce, HubSpot, Zoho CRM, Microsoft Dynamics 365.

2. Sales Automation Tools

Sales automation tools streamline repetitive tasks, such as data entry, follow-up emails, and appointment scheduling. Key benefits include:

- **Increased Productivity**: Automating routine tasks frees up time for sales professionals to focus on selling.
- **Consistency**: Ensures consistent communication and follow-up with leads.

Examples of Sales Automation Tools: Outreach, Yesware, Pipedrive.

3. Data Analytics and Reporting Tools

Data analytics tools provide valuable insights into sales performance, customer behavior, and market trends. They enable sales teams to make data-driven decisions. Key features include:

- **Performance Tracking**: Monitoring sales metrics and KPIs in real-time.
- **Customer Insights**: Analyzing customer data to identify patterns and preferences.

Popular Data Analytics Tools: Tableau, Google Analytics, Microsoft Power BI.

4. Communication and Collaboration Tools

Effective communication and collaboration are essential for sales success. These tools facilitate seamless interaction among team members and with customers. Key features include:

- **Instant Messaging**: Quick communication through platforms like Slack or Microsoft Teams.
- **Video Conferencing**: Virtual meetings with tools like Zoom or Microsoft Teams.

5. E-commerce and Sales Platforms

E-commerce platforms enable organizations to sell products and services online. They provide features for managing inventory, processing transactions, and tracking customer interactions. Key benefits include:

- **Expanded Reach**: Access to a global customer base.
- **24/7 Availability**: Customers can make purchases anytime, increasing sales opportunities.

Popular E-commerce Platforms: Shopify, WooCommerce, BigCommerce.

15.3 Implementing Sales Technology

1. Assessing Organizational Needs

Before implementing sales technology, assess the specific needs and pain points of the organization. Consider factors such as:

- **Sales Processes**: Identify areas where technology can streamline workflows.
- **Team Size**: Consider the number of users and their technological proficiency.
- **Budget**: Determine the budget available for technology investments.

2. Choosing the Right Technology

Select technologies that align with the organization's goals and needs. Conduct thorough research and evaluation of available options. Key considerations include:

- **Features and Functionality**: Ensure that the technology provides the necessary features to support sales activities.

- **User-Friendliness**: Choose technology that is easy for the sales team to adopt and use.

- **Integration Capabilities**: Ensure that the technology can integrate with existing systems and tools.

3. Training and Onboarding

Successful implementation of sales technology requires comprehensive training and onboarding for sales teams. Key steps include:

- **Creating Training Materials**: Develop user manuals, tutorials, and guides to facilitate learning.

- **Conducting Workshops**: Organize hands-on training sessions to help users familiarize themselves with the technology.

- **Providing Ongoing Support**: Offer continued support and resources to address questions and challenges.

15.4 Best Practices for Leveraging Sales Technology

1. Encourage User Adoption

Foster a culture of technology adoption within the sales team. Encourage team members to embrace new tools and demonstrate their benefits. Strategies include:

- **Highlighting Success Stories**: Share examples of how technology has improved sales outcomes.

- **Incentivizing Usage**: Consider implementing rewards or recognition programs for team members who effectively utilize technology.

2. Continuously Monitor Performance

Regularly monitor the performance of sales technologies to assess their effectiveness. Analyze data and feedback to identify areas for improvement. Key actions include:

- **Tracking Usage Metrics**: Monitor how often sales teams use the technology and its impact on performance.
- **Collecting Feedback**: Solicit feedback from users to identify challenges and areas for enhancement.

3. Stay Updated with Technological Advancements

The technology landscape is constantly evolving. Stay informed about new developments, trends, and emerging technologies that can enhance sales processes. Consider:

- **Attending Industry Conferences**: Participate in events to learn about the latest innovations in sales technology.
- **Engaging with Online Communities**: Join forums and groups to connect with other sales professionals and share insights.

15.5 Future Trends in Sales Technology

1. Artificial Intelligence (AI) and Machine Learning

AI and machine learning are transforming sales processes by automating tasks, analyzing customer data, and providing predictive analytics. These technologies enable sales teams to:

- **Personalize Customer Interactions**: Tailor messaging and offers based on customer behavior and preferences.
- **Improve Lead Scoring**: Use data-driven algorithms to prioritize leads more effectively.

2. Advanced Analytics and Big Data

The increasing availability of big data allows sales teams to gain deeper insights into customer behavior and market trends. Advanced analytics tools will enable:

- **Real-Time Decision Making**: Sales teams can make informed decisions based on up-to-date data.
- **Enhanced Customer Segmentation**: More precise targeting of marketing efforts.

3. Virtual and Augmented Reality (VR/AR)

VR and AR technologies have the potential to revolutionize customer engagement by providing immersive experiences. Sales teams can leverage these technologies for:

- **Product Demonstrations**: Offering virtual product experiences that enhance customer understanding.
- **Remote Collaboration**: Facilitating virtual meetings that simulate in-person interactions.

Leveraging technology in sales is essential for optimizing performance, enhancing customer engagement, and achieving organizational goals. By understanding the various types of sales technologies, implementing them effectively, and adhering to best practices, organizations can empower their sales teams to thrive in a competitive landscape. As technology continues to evolve, staying informed about emerging trends and innovations will be crucial for maintaining a strategic advantage in the marketplace. By embracing technological advancements, organizations can not only improve their sales processes but also foster stronger relationships with customers, ultimately driving long-term success.

Chapter 16
The Future of Sales: Trends and Predictions

As the landscape of business evolves, so too does the field of sales. The rapid advancement of technology, changing consumer behavior, and shifting market dynamics all contribute to a transformative environment for sales professionals. This chapter explores key trends shaping the future of sales, predictions for the coming years, and strategies for adapting to these changes.

16.1 Current Trends Influencing Sales

1. Increased Use of Data Analytics

Data analytics has become a cornerstone of successful sales strategies. Sales professionals increasingly rely on data to understand customer preferences, track performance, and predict future sales trends. Key aspects include:

- **Predictive Analytics**: Utilizing historical data to forecast future sales trends and customer behavior, enabling proactive decision-making.

- **Customer Insights**: Leveraging analytics to segment customers, personalize communications, and tailor offerings based on individual needs.

2. Emphasis on Customer Experience

Today's consumers expect more than just a transaction; they seek a seamless and personalized experience throughout their purchasing journey. Sales teams must focus on:

- **Personalization**: Customizing interactions and offers based on individual customer preferences and behaviors.
- **Omnichannel Engagement**: Providing a consistent experience across multiple channels, including online, in-person, and social media.

3. Remote Selling and Virtual Engagement

The COVID-19 pandemic accelerated the shift towards remote selling and virtual engagements. As businesses adapt to this new normal, sales teams must:

- **Utilize Virtual Tools**: Embrace video conferencing, virtual demos, and online collaboration tools to engage with customers effectively.
- **Adapt Communication Styles**: Develop skills for virtual communication to build rapport and trust remotely.

16.2 Emerging Technologies in Sales

1. Artificial Intelligence (AI)

AI is revolutionizing sales processes by automating tasks, enhancing lead generation, and providing deeper customer insights. Key applications include:

- **Chatbots**: AI-powered chatbots can handle customer inquiries and provide immediate support, improving response times and customer satisfaction.

- **Lead Scoring**: AI algorithms analyze data to prioritize leads based on their likelihood to convert, allowing sales teams to focus on high-potential opportunities.

2. Advanced CRM Solutions

The next generation of Customer Relationship Management (CRM) systems will incorporate AI, machine learning, and advanced analytics. Benefits include:

- **Enhanced Automation**: Automating routine tasks, such as data entry and follow-ups, freeing up time for sales professionals to focus on relationship-building.
- **Integrated Insights**: Combining data from various sources to provide comprehensive insights into customer interactions and sales performance.

3. Social Selling

Social media platforms are increasingly becoming vital tools for sales professionals. Social selling involves leveraging social media to engage with prospects, build relationships, and generate leads. Key strategies include:

- **Building a Personal Brand**: Establishing credibility and authority on social platforms to attract potential customers.
- **Engaging with Content**: Sharing valuable content and insights to foster connections and drive engagement with target audiences.

16.3 Predictions for the Future of Sales

1. Enhanced Personalization Through Technology

The future of sales will see an even greater emphasis on personalization. As technology advances, sales teams will leverage sophisticated tools to create highly tailored experiences for customers. Predictions include:

- **Hyper-Personalization**: Utilizing AI and data analytics to deliver real-time, customized recommendations and offers based on individual preferences.
- **Customer Journey Mapping**: Analyzing customer interactions across touchpoints to optimize the buying journey and enhance overall satisfaction.

2. The Rise of Subscription-Based Sales Models

Subscription-based sales models are gaining popularity across various industries, offering customers ongoing value and convenience. This trend is expected to continue, leading to:

- **Recurring Revenue Streams**: Businesses will increasingly adopt subscription models to ensure consistent revenue and foster customer loyalty.
- **Customer Retention Focus**: Sales teams will prioritize customer retention strategies to maintain subscription-based relationships.

3. Increased Focus on Ethical Selling

As consumers become more conscious of corporate responsibility and ethical practices, sales professionals will need to prioritize transparency and integrity. Predictions include:

- **Value-Based Selling**: Focusing on the values and mission of the organization to align with customers' expectations and preferences.

- **Building Trust**: Establishing long-term relationships based on trust and transparency to enhance customer loyalty.

16.4 Adapting to Change: Strategies for Sales Teams

1. Continuous Learning and Development

To thrive in the evolving sales landscape, sales professionals must commit to ongoing learning and skill development. Strategies include:

- **Embracing New Technologies**: Staying informed about the latest tools and technologies that can enhance sales processes.
- **Participating in Training Programs**: Engaging in workshops and training sessions to improve skills in areas such as digital selling, customer engagement, and data analytics.

2. Fostering a Culture of Agility

Sales teams must adopt an agile mindset to respond quickly to changing market dynamics. Key actions include:

- **Encouraging Experimentation**: Allowing team members to test new approaches and strategies without fear of failure.
- **Monitoring Market Trends**: Keeping a pulse on industry developments to proactively adapt sales strategies.

3. Collaborating Across Departments

Sales professionals should work closely with marketing, customer service, and product development teams to ensure a cohesive approach. Collaborative efforts can lead to:

- **Integrated Campaigns**: Creating campaigns that align messaging and branding across departments.
- **Holistic Customer Understanding**: Sharing insights from different teams to gain a comprehensive understanding of customer needs and preferences.

The future of sales is marked by rapid change and innovation, driven by technological advancements and evolving consumer expectations. To succeed in this dynamic landscape, sales professionals must embrace emerging technologies, prioritize customer experience, and foster a culture of continuous learning and agility. By staying informed about trends and adapting strategies accordingly, organizations can position themselves for success in an increasingly competitive marketplace. The journey ahead may be challenging, but with the right mindset and tools, sales teams can thrive and build lasting relationships with customers, ultimately driving long-term growth and success.

Appendices

Appendix A: Glossary of Psychological and Sales Terms

This glossary provides definitions of key terms related to psychology and sales, enhancing the reader's understanding of concepts discussed throughout the book.

A.1 Psychological Terms

- **Behavioral Psychology**: A branch of psychology focused on understanding and modifying observable behaviors through conditioning and reinforcement.

- **Cognitive Dissonance**: The mental discomfort experienced by a person when holding contradictory beliefs, values, or attitudes, particularly during decision-making.

- **Motivation**: The psychological process that drives individuals to take action toward achieving a goal or fulfilling a need.

- **Perception**: The process by which individuals interpret and make sense of sensory information, influencing their attitudes and behaviors.

- **Social Proof**: The phenomenon where individuals look to the behavior of others to guide their own actions, especially in uncertain situations.

A.2 Sales Terms

- **Closing**: The process of finalizing a sale, typically involving the final agreement and payment.

- **Lead**: A potential customer who has expressed interest in a product or service.

- **Objection Handling**: Techniques used by sales professionals to address and overcome customer objections or concerns during the sales process.

- **Value Proposition**: A statement that clearly outlines the benefits and value a product or service offers to customers, differentiating it from competitors.

- **Sales Funnel**: A model that represents the stages a potential customer goes through from awareness to purchase, typically including stages like awareness, interest, consideration, and conversion.

***

Appendix B: Additional Readings and Resources for Further Learning

This section lists recommended books, articles, and online resources for those interested in deepening their understanding of business psychology and sales.

B.1 Recommended Books

1. **"Influence: The Psychology of Persuasion" by Robert B. Cialdini**
    - A foundational text on the principles of influence and persuasion in sales and marketing.

2. **"Thinking, Fast and Slow" by Daniel Kahneman**
   o A comprehensive exploration of how people think and make decisions, with implications for sales strategies.

3. **"SPIN Selling" by Neil Rackham**
   o A research-based approach to selling that focuses on asking the right questions to understand customer needs.

4. **"The Challenger Sale: Taking Control of the Customer Conversation" by Matthew Dixon and Brent Adamson**
   o A look at how successful salespeople challenge customers' thinking and provide unique insights.

5. **"To Sell Is Human: The Surprising Truth About Moving Others" by Daniel H. Pink**
   o An examination of the art and science of selling, highlighting the importance of empathy and understanding.

B.2 Online Resources

- **HubSpot Academy**: Offers free courses on sales, marketing, and customer service.
- **Coursera**: Provides online courses in psychology and sales, often in collaboration with top universities.
- **Harvard Business Review**: Features articles and research on sales strategies, customer behavior, and business psychology.

- **Sales Hacker**: A community for sales professionals that provides articles, webinars, and podcasts on modern sales techniques.

***

Appendix C: Useful Sales Psychology Tools and Techniques

This appendix outlines practical tools and techniques that sales professionals can use to enhance their effectiveness through psychological principles.

C.1 Tools

1. **CRM Software (e.g., Salesforce, HubSpot)**
   - Helps manage customer relationships, track interactions, and analyze sales data to improve decision-making.
2. **Sales Enablement Platforms (e.g., Seismic, Highspot)**
   - Provides sales teams with the resources, tools, and training needed to effectively engage with prospects.
3. **Email Tracking Tools (e.g., Yesware, Boomerang)**
   - Allows sales professionals to track email opens and responses, providing insights into customer engagement.

4. **A/B Testing Tools (e.g., Optimizely, VWO)**
    - Used to test different messaging or approaches to determine which resonates best with customers.

C.2 Techniques

1. **Active Listening**
    - Engaging with customers through reflective listening to build rapport and understand their needs better.

2. **Building Rapport**
    - Establishing a connection with prospects by finding common ground and showing genuine interest in their concerns.

3. **Utilizing Storytelling**
    - Sharing relatable stories that illustrate product benefits and create emotional connections with customers.

4. **The Foot-in-the-Door Technique**
    - Starting with a small request to gain compliance, then following up with a larger request (the main sale).

5. **Reciprocity Principle**
    - Providing value upfront (such as free trials or valuable content) to encourage customers to reciprocate by making a purchase.

References

1. Cialdini, R. B. (2006). *Influence: The Psychology of Persuasion*. Harper Business.

2. Coursera. (n.d.). Online Courses in Psychology and Sales. Retrieved from https://www.coursera.org

3. Cuddy, A. J. C. (2015). *Presence: Bringing Your Boldest Self to Your Biggest Challenges*. Little, Brown and Company.

4. Danielson, C. (2016). *The Art of Selling: The Psychology of Sales and Persuasion*. Routledge.

5. Dixon, M., & Adamson, B. (2011). *The Challenger Sale: Taking Control of the Customer Conversation*. Portfolio Hardcover.

6. Fogg, B. J. (2009). *Behavior Design: A New Approach to Persuasive Technology*. Stanford University.

7. Goleman, D. (1995). *Emotional Intelligence: Why It Can Matter More Than IQ*. Bantam Books.

8. Harvard Business Review. (n.d.). Articles on Sales Strategies and Customer Behavior. Retrieved from https://hbr.org

9. Heath, C., & Heath, D. (2010). *Switch: How to Change Things When Change Is Hard*. Crown Business.

10. HubSpot Academy. (n.d.). Sales Courses and Certifications. Retrieved from https://academy.hubspot.com

11. Kahneman, D. (2011). *Thinking, Fast and Slow*. Farrar, Straus and Giroux.

12. Lencioni, P. (2002). *The Five Dysfunctions of a Team: A Leadership Fable*. Jossey-Bass.

13. Optimizely. (n.d.). A/B Testing and Experimentation Tools. Retrieved from https://www.optimizely.com

14. Pink, D. H. (2012). *To Sell Is Human: The Surprising Truth About Moving Others*. Riverhead Books.

15. Rackham, N. (1988). *SPIN Selling*. McGraw-Hill Education.

16. Sales Hacker. (n.d.). Resources for Sales Professionals. Retrieved from https://www.saleshacker.com

17. Schwartz, B. (2004). *The Paradox of Choice: Why More Is Less*. HarperCollins.

18. Seismic. (n.d.). Sales Enablement Solutions. Retrieved from https://www.seismic.com

19. Tversky, A., & Kahneman, D. (1974). "Judgment under Uncertainty: Heuristics and Biases." *Science*, 185(4157), 1124-1131.

20. Yesware. (n.d.). Email Tracking and Sales Tools. Retrieved from https://www.yesware.com

www.ingramcontent.com/pod-product-compliance
Lightning Source LLC
LaVergne TN
LVHW030322070526
838199LV00069B/6534